Federalism and Internal Conflicts

Series Editors

Soeren Keil
School of Psychology, Politics and Sociology
Canterbury Christ Church University
Canterbury, UK

Eva Maria Belser
University of Freiburg
Freiburg, Switzerland

This series engages in the discussions on federalism as a tool of internal conflict resolution. Building on a growing body of literature on the use of federalism and territorial autonomy to solve ethnic, cultural, linguistic and identity conflicts, both in the West and in non-Western countries, this global series assesses to what extent different forms of federalism and territorial autonomy are being used as tools of conflict resolution and how successful these approaches are.

We welcome proposals on theoretical debates, single case studies and short comparative pieces covering topics such as:

- Federalism and peace-making in contemporary intra-state conflicts
- The link between federalism and democratization in countries facing intra-state conflict
- Secessionism, separatism, self-determination and power-sharing
- Inter-group violence and the potential of federalism to transform conflicts
- Successes and failures of federalism and other forms of territorial autonomy in post-conflict countries
- Federalism, decentralisation and resource conflicts
- Peace treaties, interim constitutions and permanent power sharing arrangements
- The role of international actors in the promotion of federalism (and other forms of territorial autonomy) as tools of internal conflict resolution
- Federalism and state-building
- Federalism, democracy and minority protection

For further information on the series and to submit a proposal for consideration, please get in touch with Ambra Finotello ambra.finotello@palgrave.com, or series editors Soeren Keil soeren.keil@canterbury.ac.uk and Eva Maria Belser evamaria.belser@unifr.ch

More information about this series at
http://www.palgrave.com/gp/series/15730

Felix Schulte

Peace through Self-Determination

Success and Failure of Territorial Autonomy

palgrave
macmillan

Felix Schulte
Institute of Political Science
Heidelberg University
Heidelberg, Germany

Federalism and Internal Conflicts
ISBN 978-3-030-37589-8 ISBN 978-3-030-37587-4 (eBook)
https://doi.org/10.1007/978-3-030-37587-4

Cover illustration: Westend61 / Getty Images

This Palgrave Macmillan imprint is published by the registered company Springer Nature Switzerland AG.
The registered company address is: Gewerbestrasse 11, 6330 Cham, Switzerland

Acknowledgments

Writing this book would not have been possible without the outstanding support of a long list of people. First and foremost, I would like to thank Aurel Croissant, who oversaw more than three years of my doctoral research and helped me grow as a political scientist. He gave me the freedom to make my own choices and experiences, support when I needed it, and direction when I risked losing sight of the bigger picture. I would like to thank numerous colleagues and friends, inside and outside the University of Heidelberg, for the many inspiring discussions, constructive feedback, and the friendly working environment. You know who you are: writing this book would have been a lot more difficult without your sympathetic ears over lunch or dinner, welcome distractions, and supportive messages. My thanks also go to the participants of various colloquia at the Institute of Political Science for their helpful comments and suggestions. The Graduate Academy of the University of Heidelberg enabled me to participate in various conferences and workshops at which I had the opportunity to present this project. My work has benefited greatly from methodological feedback made by Eva Thomann and Claude Rubinson. An enriching experience was my research stay at the Institute for Minority Rights at the European Academy in Bolzano. Elisabeth Alber, Sergiu Constantin, Stephen Larin, Alexandra Tomaselli, and Marc Röggla have made this a memorable life experience for me. My sincere gratitude goes to Sia S. Åkermark and Sarah Stephan, who have significantly influenced my first steps in autonomy research during my visit at the Åland Islands Peace Institute in Mariehamn. Sloane Kozyak and Ria Baumann have been careful and patient proofreaders and have significantly improved the quality of the text. My sisters Anna Lisa, Henriette, and Pauline and a number of wonderful friends both within and outside academia have also been a constant source of advice and support throughout the past years. I am deeply grateful to Johanna for her untiring patience and always believing in me—and for constantly reminding me that there is a beautiful life outside of academia. Most of all, I owe a debt of gratitude to my parents for their unwavering encouragement and support over the years. This is for both of you.

Heidelberg,
Christmas 2019

Contents

List of Figures

List of Tables

CHAPTER 1

Introduction: Ethnic Conflict Regulation Through Territorial Autonomy

Ethnic group's demands for increased autonomy or secession have been a cause for more than a third of all civil wars since the end of the Second World War. To simultaneously appease highly emotional separatists and maintain sovereignty and territorial integrity, governments often offer forms of self-government. The number of ethnic groups that have been granted meaningful autonomy rights has steadily increased since the end of the Second World War and has almost doubled after the fall of the Iron Curtain.[1] However, territorial autonomy is obviously no panacea for regulating ethnic self-determination conflicts. Self-rule for the Chittagong Hill Tracts in Bangladesh, Mindanao in the Philippines, or Jammu and Kashmir in India has not led to peaceful interethnic coexistence between majorities and ethnic minorities, while autonomy reforms have significantly reduced ethnic tensions in other places, such as Gagauzia in Moldova or Bougainville in Papua New Guinea. How can this variance in outcomes be explained?

Despite increased scholarly interest in recent years, answers to the question of how and under what circumstances a conflictual relationship between ethnic groups can be institutionally transformed into a peaceful coexistence remain vague, and at times inconsistent. Previous research focuses primarily on the question of whether specific institutions, such as grand coalitions, veto rights, electoral reforms, or, most prominently, decentralization and the strengthening of subnational governance, are

[1] Sambanis, Germann, and Schädel, "SDM."

F. Schulte, *Peace through Self-Determination*, Federalism and Internal Conflicts,
https://doi.org/10.1007/978-3-030-37587-4_1

appropriate instruments to prevent or reduce ethnic tensions or whether they are destined to fail because of inherent weaknesses. Current autonomy research can be broadly divided into two camps: those who believe that autonomy solutions are a valuable option and those who do not. The proponents believe that the transfer of autonomy rights is a suitable solution for multiethnic societies and argue that territorial autonomy arrangements function as an institutional bargaining arena that enhances the chance of a peaceful conflict regulation.[2] Post-conflict territorial self-government reforms follow the logic of separating groups by distributing political powers. This is expected to reduce the stakes of competition for state power and can even, as some argue, strengthen the rule of law and create good governance.[3] First and foremost, autonomy reforms ensure official minority recognition and substantial self-government guaranteed for ethnic groups, which may dampen separatist desires. At the same time, territorial autonomy takes into account sovereignty and territorial integrity as key interests of a nation-state.

According to critics, proponents underestimate certain practical realities on the ground as such an institutional balance is often an unhappy compromise between ethnic groups that are pursuing higher levels of self-determination and central governments that are seeking to re-centralize powers.[4] The highly asymmetric and exclusive character of territorial autonomy leads to a strong accentuation of ethnic differences. This, in turn, facilitates centrifugal activities, as empowerment equips ethnic leaders with necessary resources, strengthens social cohesion, and creates optimal conditions for collective action: "While [autonomy] provides national minorities with a workable alternative to secession, it also helps to make secession a more realistic alternative".[5] Establishing a local authority homogenizes on a sub-state level, when ethnic leaders who have endured

[2] Lapidoth, Autonomy. Flexible Solutions to Ethnic Conflicts; Nordquist, "Autonomy as a Conflict-Solving Mechanism-an Overview"; Hartzell and Hoddie, "Institutionalizing Peace: Power Sharing and Post-Civil War Conflict Management"; Schneckener and Wolff, *Managing and Settling Ethnic Conflicts: Perspectives on Successes and Failures in Europe, Africa and Asia*; Åkermark, "Internal Self-Determination and the Role of Territorial Autonomy as a Tool for the Resolution of Ethno-Political Disputes."

[3] Ghai, "Autonomy as a Strategy for Diffusing Conflict"; Gagnon and Keating, *Political Autonomy and Divided Societies*; Ganguly, *Autonomy and Ethnic Conflict in South and South-East Asia*.

[4] Hale, "Divided We Stand: Institutional Sources of Ethnofederal State Survival and Collapse."

[5] Kymlicka, "Multiculturalism and Minority Rights: West and East," 2.

exclusion become eager nation-builders themselves. Since autonomous territories are home to other ethnic minorities, further tensions and political instability are created. A common concern in both scientific and political discourses is that of a contagion effect. If the central state grants autonomy to a group, demands by other groups for self-determination will follow and ultimately will lead to the disintegration of the entire state.[6]

Although we find empirical evidence for some of the theoretical arguments, a too pessimistic view does not stand up to scrutiny. No empirical study, so far, finds a robust causal relationship between post-conflict autonomy reforms and the re-occurrence of violent secessionist conflict. Where autonomy reforms have been implemented to end ethnic conflict, many have succeeded in at least reducing violence to a manageable level. In the recent past, some authors have tried to rekindle the stalled debate between proponents and critics by taking a more nuanced view on the autonomy-conflict nexus. Daftary or Cederman et al. conclude that conflict regulation through autonomy does not fail because of the type of institutional reform, but rather because of its delayed implementation.[7] Siroky's and Cuffe's findings indicate that the probability of secessionist conflict is only high when groups have lost their historic special status.[8] Abushov argues that the success of conflict regulation through territorial autonomy depends primarily on the nature of the intrastate conflict. He concludes that success is likely if autonomy serves to express cultural identity more strongly, whereas failure is to be expected when it comes to correcting historic injustices about the belonging of the territory.[9] Anderson and Costa find the balance of power between different levels of government decisive.[10] Danspeckgruber or Walsh highlight the necessity of domestic and international guarantees for the special status for overcoming the inherent lack of trust between groups and preventing instability.[11]

[6] Saideman, "Is Pandora's Box Half Empty or Half Full? The Limited Virulence of Secessionism and the Domestic Sources of Disintegration"; Walter, *Reputation and Civil War*; Forsberg, "Do Ethnic Dominoes Fall?"

[7] Daftary, "Territorial Autonomy as a Response to Violent Self-Determination Conflicts: 'Too Little, Too Late'?" Cederman et al., "Territorial Autonomy in the Shadow of Conflict: Too Little, Too Late?"

[8] Siroky and Cuffe, "Lost Autonomy, Nationalism and Separatism."

[9] Abushov, "Autonomy as a Possible Solution to Self-Determination Disputes: Does It Really Work?"

[10] Anderson and Costa, "Survival of the Fittest."

[11] Danspeckgruber, "Self-Governance plus Regional Integration: A Possible Solution to Self-Determination Conflicts"; Walsh, *Territorial Self-Government as a Conflict Management Tool.*

While these works provide for a differentiated perspective on the conflict-regulating potential of territorial autonomy, a general shift in the research interest "away from the pros and cons [...] towards an effort to explain *what factors* influence the stability and longevity of autonomy solutions has, however, not taken place so far".[12]

Can autonomies end intrastate conflicts between ethnic groups or does the granting of self-determination rights result in violent secessionist conflict? Research efforts to answer this general question have not provided conclusive evidence so far—but only because this question cannot be answered *as such*. Since there are successful examples, such as the Åland Islands in Finland, Gagauzia in Moldova, or South Tyrol in Italy, as well as obviously failed cases, the discussion addressing the general role of autonomy solutions in ethnic conflicts is not a very fruitful one. The implementation of territorial self-governance does not necessarily lead to lasting peace, just like how violent conflicts are not an inevitable consequence. Both institutional successes and failures do not occur in a vacuum. They rather depend on both the right choice of institutional set-up, as well as favorable and unfavorable circumstances strengthening or weakening the implemented rules.

The Argument: Ethnic Recognition Matters

Post-conflict reforms are generally considered successful if tensions do not re-escalate and all relevant actors regard implemented institutions as the only rules in town. This book argues that in the specific context of ethnic self-determination conflicts, institutional success depends on whether post-conflict institutions work toward the fundamental requirement of ethnic peace, namely the mutual recognition of majority and minority, both being part of a national demos.

The deeper reasons for this lie in human nature as a zoon politikon and social being. It is a well-known fact that everyone has an idea not only of herself, that is, a personal identity, but also of her belonging to social collectives and thus has a social identity. Social Identity Theory tells us that people generally strive for recognition of their personal as well as social identities and cannot simply be persuaded to give up the satisfaction of this

[12] Åkermark, "Internal Self-Determination and the Role of Territorial Autonomy as a Tool for the Resolution of Ethno-Political Disputes," 17.

basic human need. Ethnic groups whose social identity is based on life-determining cultural elements, namely language, tradition, religion, and historicity, have a particularly high need for recognition through relevant others. Regardless of physical resources or political power, ethnic identity groups will agitate, though with different political strategies, for the satisfaction of those human needs.

As ethnic self-determination conflicts are essentially cultural identity conflicts, mutual ethnic recognition proves to be, in turn, the all-important key for successful ethnic conflict regulation, which can serve as a normative point of orientation for different multicultural policies. This book argues that territorial autonomy arrangements provide the basis for mutual recognition through a substantial degree of self-rule and a guaranteed special status for an ethnic settlement area. This makes them a highly suitable institutional option for transforming antagonistic relations between majority and minority into peaceful interethnic cohabitation. However, while territorial autonomy creates the supportive legal framework, mutual recognition is anything but easy to achieve in the context of highly emotional self-determination conflict and needs to be understood as a fragile and highly context-dependent process. Successful conflict-regulating autonomies follow three sequential steps:

To start, the autonomy reforms must be widely accepted by the majority and minority groups as the best available option. Ethnic leaders support institutional reforms if reforms credibly promise a considerable degree of self-rule and, consequently, political power. The chances of achieving at least partial independence from the influence of the central government are considered higher than the chances of non-cooperative strategies being successful. At the same time, though, the political survival of ethnic leaders depends on the support of ordinary followers. Group members follow moderate and autonomy-friendly politicians and parties when they expect institutional reforms to improve their daily lives and when they have a credible commitment that self-determination rights and cultural protection will continue in the future and will not be replaced by majority dominance and assimilative re-centralization efforts.

While such general acceptance of autonomy reforms is a fundamental prerequisite for autonomy consolidation, it is not wholly sufficient for achieving a state of mutual recognition. Based on consociational considerations, the second step requires rapprochement processes on elite level. Suitable cooperation opportunities available to the actors, incentives, and pressures to stick to the agreements allow leaders to cooperate and compromise. Successful cooperation at the political level may then trickle down and send decisive signals for rapprochement processes on mass level. This ultimately enables broad mutual recognition between majority and minority and ensures the long-term success of post-conflict autonomy reforms.

Successful autonomy solutions tell us that this process does not occur in a vacuum but can only take place and ultimately lead to long-term consolidation if various favorable framework conditions initiate and support this process of ethnic recognition. It is only the interplay of specific, recognition-promoting factors, both structural and actor centered, that allows territorial self-governance to unfold its positive effect on interethnic cohabitation. From a theoretical perspective, the basic acceptance of autonomy reforms as a first step toward ethnic recognition depends crucially on a high degree of transferred self-determination competencies, which provides ethnic elites with considerable political power, as well as on their chosen conflict strategy beforehand. If mere demands for autonomy have been made, the strategic objective of the self-determination movement and the institutional result achieved are coherent. If this goal has been pursued largely peacefully, there is a good chance that elites will be able to reach agreement on implementation, adhere to negotiated deals, and engage in deeper cooperation. In the case of violent secessionist demands, the signs for autonomy success are far less promising.

It is a robust empirical finding of peace research that highly asymmetric relationships between social groups can have a strong negative effect on peaceful coexistence. Persistent group grievances enhance in-group favoritism and provoke counter-reactions against out-groups, which may spur separatist desires and make unconventional strategies a viable option. Consequently, the absence of strong social and economic horizontal inequalities between majority and minority makes autonomy consolidation a more likely outcome. While a high degree of self-determination, non-violent demands for limited sovereignty, and a low degree of horizontal inequalities theoretically provide good reasons why ethnic minorities are willing to invest in autonomy arrangements over the long run, a comprehensive explanation must also consider the supply side. Cooperation efforts between elites as the subsequent step require further recognition-promoting structural and actor-centered factors, which are found in inclusive state institutions, minority-friendly parties, and international support. While inclusive institutions such as proportional representation or parliamentary systems offer suitable negotiation forums for elite cooperation, their positive impact hinges strongly on the actors involved. In contrast to right-wing nationalist or populist parties, mainstream right- or left-wing parties are ideologically capable of making multiculturalism a part of their political agenda and of perceiving ethnic minorities as part of the demos. This is an important prerequisite for enabling rapprochement at the elite level and for both sides to accept a special status for a minority territory.

A closer look at success stories makes it clear that a peaceful and long-term regulation of highly emotional ethnic conflicts can hardly be achieved without the support of external actors. This study shows that external mediation as well as the international integration of autonomous regions in policy networks substantially help to break the logic of ethnic polarization and to reorganize interethnic relations by offering communication channels and credible guarantees for both sides.

Just as important and in need of explanation as the question of autonomy consolidation is the question of the failure of autonomy systems. According to the theoretical assumptions, autonomy solutions fail to pacify self-determination conflicts if the process of mutual recognition is not initiated or interrupted at an early stage. This is the case when the powers transferred to regional institutions are too weak, inequalities create new group grievances, there are only insufficient opportunities for political cooperation and the majority and minority cannot count on external support to reorganize their relationship with each other. If autonomy reforms coincide with such unfavorable circumstances, territorial self-government arrangements are hardly capable of surviving the post-conflict period and the re-occurrence of ethnic violence is a likely consequence.

The book complements existing research in three important ways. First, it examines territorial autonomies and thus takes into account an institution that is particularly relevant from an empirical point of view and that has, in contrast to integrative forms of power sharing or electoral reforms so far been less the focus of political science research. While research has long confirmed the peace-promoting, or at least conflict-dampening, effect of peaceful strategies, inclusive institutions, and low inequalities, it is poorly understood how these conditions, as intervening variables, lead to the success or failure of specific post-conflict institutions. The book presents causal models for both possible outcomes. For this purpose, the study combines institutionalist approaches with socio-psychological theories, thus providing a highly comprehensive and micro-level explanation. Third, and most importantly, the study does not ask for statistical effects of single variables, but whether exogenous factors are causally relevant for autonomy success and failure in the sense of necessary and sufficient conditions and whether and how these factors interact with each other. While a plethora of variables more or less strongly influence highly complex and case-specific phenomena like autonomy consolidation, it is, as this study shows, a rather modest configuration of six necessary conditions, which are jointly sufficient to explain autonomy success, while a combination of just four factors is sufficient to explain autonomy failures.

The Organization of the Book

The book rolls the field up from behind by first discussing the role of ethnic identity in political conflicts. The advent of the modern nation-state has led to the alienation and marginalization of many cultural minorities. In many cases, the resulting self-determination conflicts make it necessary to turn away from the idea of a unitary and homogeneous nation-state to prevent full on state-collapse. Based on consociational literature, minority rights, executive power sharing, and territorial autonomy are identified as potential managing institutions which, at least theoretically, enable ethnic recognition. Due to the vagueness of the term "autonomy" in political science literature, the first chapter deals with constitutive elements of the concept to be investigated. On this basis, a sample of 19 conflict-regulating territorial autonomies implemented between 1922 and 2009 is selected. To assess the outcome condition, I present a comprehensive success analysis based on three criteria, conflict intensity, institutional sustainability, and public acceptance, whereas each case is classified as being successful, partly successful, partly failed, or failed. Chapter 2 then presents the theoretical model of autonomy success and failure. Building on the key assumption of Social Identity Theory, I identify mutual recognition of cultural identities as the focal point for autonomy consolidation and outline the three-step social mechanism toward ethnic recognition mentioned above. In a second step, the theoretically most relevant success factors are selected and the expectations regarding their causal effect on autonomy consolidation are presented. The study focuses initially on three structural conditions, namely the degree of autonomy, democracy, and international integration, and four actor-centered factors, namely conflict strategy, social and economic inequalities, and the engagement of international organizations.

In the first empirical step, which is conducted in Chap. 3, it is examined whether the identified conditions contribute to autonomy success in their presence and whether or not their absence appears in cases of autonomy failure. Since it is expected that it is not a single condition, but a specific contextual pattern which produces the outcomes, Qualitative Comparative Analysis (QCA) is applied as a case-sensitive method which takes equifinality and causal complexity into account.

In order to enhance the explanatory range of the theoretical models, six additional identity-relevant conditions are included in the empirical analysis. An institutional model containing the conditions of a proportional electoral system, decentralization, and rule of law in addition to an actor-specific model containing the conditions of the existence of nationalist parties in the central government, diaspora groups, and ethnic fractionalization are also analyzed set-theoretically. Finally, all empirically relevant factors are combined into two process models, each of which explains success and failure of post-conflict autonomy reforms. To increase confidence in the QCA results, I conduct several robustness tests with different data and calibrations.

In a final step, it is tested whether the postulated three-stage mechanism of recognition is actually initiated and supported by the interplay of the identified conditions. To reconstruct the hypothesized underlying causal mechanisms between the conditions and the consolidation outcome, I conduct theory-testing process-tracing on two typical cases of the sample for each consolidation outcome: Italy's South Tyrol region as successfully consolidated regional autonomy and the failure of reforms for Bangladesh's Chittagong Hill Tracts. Both case studies provide evidence for the empirical models and the causal effect of the identified configuration of conditions. The final chapter discusses important contributions and draws some key conclusions.

Setting the Context: Ethnic Self-determination Conflicts

All considerations made in this study are based on one basic assumption: conflicts as social interactions are changeable. The term conflict refers to an incompatibility with regard to socially relevant goods that exists between at least two directly involved conflict parties and is carried out by observable conflict measures. These lie outside of established and accepted rules and regulatory procedures. This study distinguishes between five different conflict intensity levels: a dispute (level 1) is a domestic conflict that exists entirely without resorting to the use or threat of violence. In a non-violent crisis (level 2), conflict parties threaten to use violence. If individual acts of violence take place, a conflict is characterized as a violent crisis (level 3). Level 3 violence is limited and does not inflict massive damage on the opponent. If there are regularly planned, violent attacks, the conflict becomes a limited war (level 4). In a war (level 5), military operations are carried out systematically and extensively.[13]

Several issues form common political goals of conflict actors such as national or international power, subnational predominance, secession, ideology, territory, or natural resources. In a significant proportion of domestic conflicts, we observe that the conflict issue itself is less important than what is actually at stake for the actors involved. Conflicts over political or cultural self-determination revolve around a general disagreement between cultural groups with claims to self-determination and the central government regarding the political status of that ethnic group. Such groups seek to gain greater power and control over their own political and cultural affairs or independence from their host states that often refuse to meet these demands. At the extreme, groups such as the Kurds, Oromo, or Abkhaz demand their own sovereign state. Ethnic self-determination conflicts are at their core identity conflicts. They are not primarily based on what the conflicting parties want, or say they want, but what they are—or believe they are.

The predominant source of social identity is the nation. Nations, as well as ethnic groups, are identity groups which both proclaim their homogeneity and we-feeling inwardly and outwardly. Group homogeneity is, however, not something natural, but a social-intellectual construction.[14] National or ethnic identity does not exist in itself, as once suggested by primordialists or perennialists, but only to the extent that individuals identify with certain cultural elements and participate in cultural communication processes. Historically, the perceived homogeneity is a product of power, created by a process that brought the nation into a political form—the nation-state. For nation-states to emerge, de facto social heterogeneity had to be homogenized. Unification is successful, on the one hand, due to physical power. On the other hand, nationalism creates homogeneity through cultural power. Discursive negotiation processes are usually dominated by a powerful group. This group, often eponymous for the

[13] Trinn and Wencker, "Introducing the Heidelberg Approach to Conflict Research."
[14] Anderson, *Imagined Communities.*

nation, determines which holidays are celebrated and which languages are taught.

Starting from the French Revolution, the nation-state became the dominant political model of order spreading its credo across the globe: One state, one nation, one people. Every state, according to this ideal, endeavors to create a "national" distinct culture on its territory and the people as a body of citizens should form a nation and each nation seeks to expand its cultural unity to a political unity. This notion of congruence of ethnos and demos offered a new emotional anchor and orientation framework after the abolition of religion as the dominant interpretive ideal. The idea of the nation as an extended family of shared identity and solidarity made the new states politically, economically, and militarily the most powerful actors on the global stage and started a wave of state-building that swept away the old empires and dynastic kingdoms and radically altered the face of the global order.[15]

While the ages of nationalism begin as a tale of democracy and the victory of the common people against the rulers of the ancient régime, it transforms into something completely different with xenophobic and illiberal movements assimilating, marginalizing or even expelling non-national others. From the perspective of those minority groups that were unable to build their own viable governance unit, such as the Bretons, Kurds, or Sorbs, the nationalist credo becomes no less than a threat to their social identity and cultural survival. With the increasing number of independent nation-states in the twentieth century, more and more minority groups felt no longer part of their host country, demanding independence, a merger with a kin state, or cultural autonomy. Those that could manage to occupy a seat in the multinational game seek to maintain their political and cultural dominance and to avoid the break-up of "their" nation-state.

If groups perceive their political status as being inequitable, this provides a causal explanation for violent group behavior, as individuals tend to direct actions against the trigger of frustration.[16] It is this discrepancy between what is desired and what has been achieved, relative deprivation, that causes disappointment that can easily be instrumentalized by

[15] Wimmer, *Waves of War. Nationalism, State Formation, and Ethnic Exclusion in the Modern World.*

[16] Dollard et al., Frustration and Aggression; Petersen, *Understanding Ethnic Violence: Fear, Hatred, and Resentment in Twentieth-Century Eastern Europe.*

nationalist demagogues.[17] While ethnic identity is not political in itself, it can easily be politicized. The social glue that holds the collective together already exists and is extremely robust. Necessary networks are either already available or easy to set up, which makes collective action problems comparatively easy to overcome. Many cases have shown that ethnic elites and parties can often rely on the moral, financial, and material support of non-fighting members. The reason is that in ethnic conflicts, individuals have a high personal interest in restoring or maintaining group status. The defeat of one's own group inevitably means the devaluation of one's own culture and one's own identity. The high amount of emotionality explains why in 2018, nearly half of all autonomy and secessionist conflicts worldwide saw the use of violence.[18]

Ethnic wars in Bosnia, Rwanda, and elsewhere have made peacebuilders become increasingly engaged in institutional reforms as a promising medication to foster the non-violent management of intrastate conflicts and have stimulated a lively debate in academia. Scholars have, based on the seminal works by Lijphart, Horowitz, or Sisk, intensively discussed how institutions can reduce the risk of renewed violence by shaping the incentives of actors, constraining their actions, and creating stimuli for moderate and cooperative behavior.[19] Although there is general agreement on the importance of post-conflict institutional design, it remains debated which institutions perform best in terms of peace and democracy and under which circumstances these intertwined goals are easiest to achieve. While some approaches seem to have worked in regulating ethnic tensions, others seem to be at odds with realities on the ground. The ongoing debate can be traced back to one fundamental question: is it better to recognize and accommodate ethnic cleavages or is it better to deny or overcome ethnicity as a factor in politics?

As the centripetalist school argues, the best way to manage shattered group relations is by diluting the zero-sum character of politics in deeply divided societies and putting institutional incentives for cross-ethnic behavior in its place.[20] Advocates recommend preferential electoral rules

[17] Gurr, *Why Men Rebel.*

[18] Heidelberg Institute for International Conflict Research, "Conflict Barometer 2018."

[19] Lijphart, "Constitutional Choices for New Democracies"; Horowitz, A Democratic South Africa? Sisk, "Electoral System Choice in South Africa: Implications for Intergroup Moderation."

[20] Horowitz, Ethnic Groups in Conflict; Sisk, "Electoral System Choice in South Africa: Implications for Intergroup Moderation"; Reilly, *Democracy in Divided Societies.*

such as Alternative Vote or Single Transferable Vote, which makes vote-seeking politicians reciprocally dependent on the votes of group members other than their own and fosters the development of poly-ethnic and centrist parties, which are capable of making cross-ethnic appeals.

In contrast, consociationalists highlight the importance of managing institutions, which take group cleavages into account, encourage cooperation and compromise, and enable groups to re-structure their relationships with each other. Ethnic identities are a social construct—but nonetheless an extremely stable and powerful idea that is not easily overcome. This is particularly true when highly emotional conflicts over self-determination and cultural identity have already escalated. Then successful vote pooling through electoral systems that offer appropriate incentives for politicians to campaign for the votes of rival groups is hardly a promising undertaking. Centripetalist incentives expect benefits of aggregation—of votes and opinions and are thus essentially majoritarian in nature. But it is, as outlined above, the very dominance of majorities that produces group grievances and provokes counter-reactions from marginalized minorities. For this reason, in many cases it is inevitable to recognize group identities on an institutional basis by sharing or dividing political power between rival ethnic groups.

Managing Institutions: Sharing or Dividing Power

Consociational theory distinguishes between three more or less intertwined managing institutions, namely minority rights, executive power sharing, and territorial autonomy, which allow for ethnic recognition, albeit to varying degrees, and thus fulfill the central requirement as recognition-supportive institutional frameworks. Minority rights are group-based positive or negative rights, aiming to protect the language, religions, or customs of a specific cultural identity group. Today, in many states, at least de jure rudimentary minority rights apply, which are particularly important for dispersed groups lacking a concentrated settlement pattern, such as Jews, Roma, or Sámi. Minority rights can contribute to peaceful ethnic coexistence in situations where governments have to deal with ethnic cleavages or wish to develop pluralistic democracy by promoting cultural diversity as an added value. Minority rights do not imply self-governance and hence do not require a transfer of legislative rights by a central government. Since they are not empowering but merely protective in nature, neither high financial contributions from the central level nor a territorial re-organization of the state as in the case of decentralization or devolution are necessary. Minority rights are the easiest managing institution to implement because they are the least costly for a central state. They can be established regardless of the number, size, and settlement pattern of ethnic groups. However, when ethnic groups have strong self-determination claims, protective minority rights appear to be an inadequate response for regulating severe intergroup tensions. While minority rights are not a suitable option for regulating violent ethnic conflicts, they belong to the ensemble of managing institutions because they are, in a way, the basis and minimum standard for other institutional arrangements, such as territorial self-governance or power sharing.

Different forms of political power sharing are part of many peace agreements and have been applied to ease ethnic tensions in some of the world's most deeply divided places. The question of how ethnic identities can be institutionally recognized is answered as simple as plausible: power is shared, and all relevant groups are given a guaranteed stake in central decision-making processes. Lijphart, Lehmbruch, and other pioneers of power sharing theory saw such institutional arrangements primarily as a way of organizing and stabilizing democracy in heterogeneous societies.[21] Whereas the conventional form of democracy is based on majority rule and is inherently power-concentrating, consociational arrangements include all relevant segments of society in decision-making processes through executive power sharing among a grand coalition, proportional representation of major groups in elected and appointed office, minority veto in government decision-making, and cultural autonomy for minority groups.

While it was initially developed as a democracy theory, consociationalism raised enormous interest among peace researchers. With this thematic extension, the concept lost its clear defining attributes, so that today many different arrangements are titled "power sharing" in literature. Some scholars study particular institutions such as electoral rules, while others argue that power can be shared not only politically and include military,

[21] Lehmbruch, *Proporzdemokratie. Politisches System und Politische Kultur in der Schweiz und in Österreich*; Lijphart, *The Politics of Accommodation. Pluralism and Democracy in the Netherlands*; Lijphart, *Patterns of Democracy. Government Forms and Performance in Thirty-Six Countries*; Armingeon, "The Effects of Negotiation Democracy"; Norris, *Driving Democracy. Do Power-Sharing Institutions Work?*

economic, and territorial power sharing in their studies.[22] Despite the contested attributes, proponents formulate rather similar expectations regarding the positive effects of power sharing on peace processes which are mostly derived from its theoretical roots: making all significant actor's stakeholders in decision-making processes provides a strong enticement for politicians to accept the legitimacy of the rules of the game. Sharing power sets incentives for cooperative behavior, which tempers extreme demands and encourages democratic bargaining and political compromises. In the second stage of the process, leaders then may promote conciliation and tolerance among their followers at the mass level.

A closer look on empirical examples of post-conflict power sharing such as Burundi, Bosnia-Herzegovina, or Liberia, however, lowers overly optimistic expectations. The reason is that post-conflict power sharing always entails a "pact with the devil", as Spears puts it.[23] The cooperation partners are not ordinary political opponents, but ethnic groups that are often unwilling to govern a state to which they feel they do not belong and which may even have brutally fought each other. The Achilles heel of power sharing is the constant willingness of all actors involved to cooperate and compromise. If there is no such basic willingness, sharing power may not produce cooperation but further tensions, if ethnic leaders abuse their right of veto to assert their own interests.

Power sharing is an institutional option worth considering whenever several groups with at least a rudimentary national identity compete for state power, such as Bosniaks, Croats, and Serbs in Bosnia and Herzegovina or Hutu and Tutsi in Burundi. However, in most ethnic self-determination conflicts, the situation is quite different when a numerically small group without a sense of belonging to the nation-state fights for political autonomy or independence.

Then dividing political power between the center and one or more substate regions within the framework of territorial autonomy is a more promising strategy. Consociationalism is based on the idea of shared power and political inclusion, but also includes autonomy rights for groups. In addition, territorial autonomy implies that political power is shared

[22] Mattes and Savun, "Fostering Peace After Civil War: Commitment Problems and Agreement Design"; Hartzell and Hoddie, "The Art of the Possible"; Ottmann and Vüllers, "The Power-Sharing Event Dataset (PSED): A New Dataset on the Promises and Practices of Power-Sharing in Post-Conflict Countries."

[23] Spears, "Africa. The Limits of Power-Sharing," 127.

between different state levels or that legislative powers are exercised jointly. This theoretical ambiguity has led to some conceptual vagueness, as many consociationalists make no clear differentiation between power sharing and territorial autonomy and tend to classify empirical cases as forms of "complex", "dispersive", or "territorial" power sharing.[24]

Power sharing refers to a division of power by *integrating* segments of society into centers of political decision-making. Territorial self-governance, on the other hand, means the division of power by *distributing* powers among multiple centers of political decision-making. While power sharing aims at political inclusion, autonomy works in the opposite direction by distributing power away from the central state. This integrative-distributive difference in the "kinetics" of power is crucial as it highlights that power sharing and territorial self-governance are two different options of post-conflict institutional engineering which are based on a different functioning logic.

If the heart piece of the managing institution is a specific political pact about sharing political power between former conflicting parties, I refer to post-conflict institutional reforms as being power sharing if they provide for a joint executive coalition government. Is the central purpose of institutional reforms to guarantee a special status for a sub-state region with legislative powers, a case is defined as territorial autonomy. In some cases, such as in Brčko District (Bosnia and Herzegovina), Northern Ireland (United Kingdom), or South Tyrol (Italy), the specific context of ethnic conflict and the existence of second-order minorities have necessitated a combination of territorial autonomy and forms of subnational power sharing. From an empirical point of view, however, this is a rather rare phenomenon. The concert of the managing institutions can be illustrated as follows (Fig. 1.1).

Whereas power sharing arrangements are based on making compromises on the policy level, territorial autonomy defines an institutional compromise of a very fundamental nature, based on the key goals of the actors involved. Dividing power limits cooperation between state and autonomous institutions to defined policy areas, which reduces the danger of mutual blockades and political standstill. For ethnic parties and leaders, the fulfillment of the demands for identity protection and guaranteed self-rule is the strongest argument for investing in autonomy reforms. For its

[24] Wolff, "Conflict Management in Divided Societies"; Hartzell and Hoddie, "The Art of the Possible"; Graham, Miller, and Strøm, "Safeguarding Democracy."

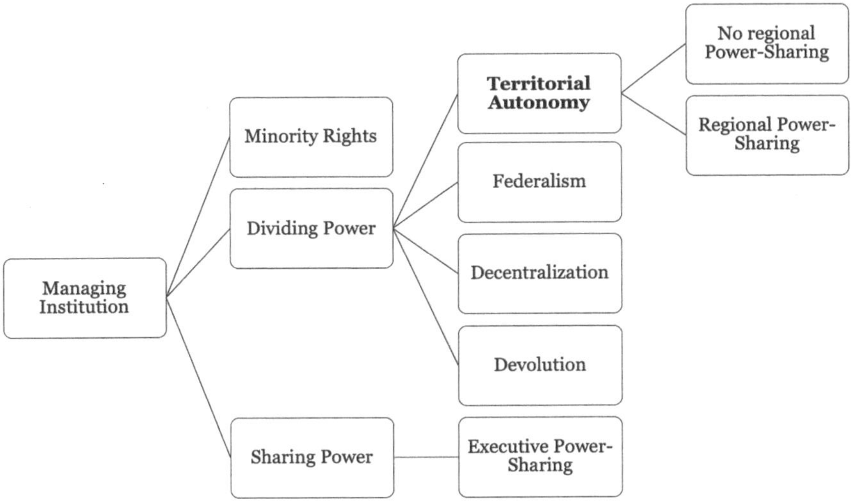

Fig. 1.1 Managing institutions. (*Source*: Own illustration)

part, the central state retains its sovereignty, territorial integrity and, to a large extent, also its cultural dominance. Critical powers such as citizenship, foreign and security policy remain in the hands of the central government. In the past, some governments have presented autonomy reforms as far-reaching concessions on their part, with the aim of enhancing their international reputation and effectively discrediting future secessionist efforts at an early stage.

Territorial self-government is the most extensive institutionalization of ethnic recognition through a guaranteed special status, including regional governments and assemblies and a considerable degree of self-rule—and thus a suitable tool for the peaceful settlement of majority-minority conflicts in deeply divided nation-states. Obviously, however, autonomy reforms do not unfold their conflict-regulating potential under all circumstances, but sometimes end in even more bloody secessionist conflicts, when, for example, ethnic leaders misuse the empowerment to manipulate the institutional reforms, and move the compromise solution in the direction which they favor, meaning more self-rule or even full independence, again bringing them into conflict with the central government. Which circumstances are needed to achieve a functioning balance between center and periphery and to create a fertile breeding ground for autonomy consolidation? Under which conditions does the vicious circle of ethnic violence persist and cause post-conflict autonomy solutions to fail? Before answering these critical questions, we first turn to the conceptualization of the object of investigation and the case selection.

Conceptualizing Territorial Autonomy

Composed of autos (gr. self) and nomos (gr. law, rule), autonomy describes the right to make or to live by one's own laws. While in the early days autonomy was equated with sovereignty, it was Thucydides who began to use the term merely to describe the limited self-determination of a community within a larger polis. Although the rights granted for the exercise of self-determination must not be affected, the legal framework created for this purpose cannot be defined by those concerned themselves. This modern understanding of political autonomy encompasses a broad spectrum of empirical cases, of which, however, not all that are labeled autonomous actually are, such as the Tibet Autonomous Region, or Russia's Autonomous Republics.

As already indicated in Fig. 1.1, the conceptualization of territorial autonomy requires a clear distinction not only from forms of political power sharing but also from various forms of vertical power division. Forms of vertical power division can be differentiated essentially based on three dimensions: (1) the standard-symmetrical or the non-standard asymmetrical character of a subnational entity, (2) the degree of self-rule, and (3) the existence of constitutional guarantees for the status of the region in question. Territorial self-governance usually takes a symmetric form in the sense that a country's territory is entirely covered by the same type of standard entity. If these subnational entities enjoy a high level of executive and legislative powers, the institutional arrangement is usually

Table 1.1 Forms of territorial self-government

	Decentralization	*Devolution*	*Federalism*	*Autonomy*
Standard vs. non-standard	Standard	Standard	Standard	Non-standard
Weak vs. strong self-rule	Weak	Strong	Strong	Strong
Guaranteed vs. non-guaranteed	No guarantee	No guarantee	Guarantee	Guarantee

referred to as federalism. If symmetrical standard regions enjoy only a low degree of self-governance, decentralization is the appropriate term. The degree of self-rule can be determined whether a regional government has law-making powers and may adopt laws in defined areas that may differ from national legislation or whether it only has regulatory self-administrative rights.[25] A further distinction can be made with regard to whether the existence or degree of self-governance of a standard or non-standard region is guaranteed by law, for example through an entrenchment in the state's constitution, or whether the status can be revoked by the central government. If symmetric standard units with a high degree of self-government lack such a legal guarantee, the term devolution usually applies (Table 1.1).

Autonomous regions are one-of-a-kind entities with a special status and thus strongly asymmetrical elements, which usually break the centralized order of unitary states. Due to their non-standard character combined with strong self-rule powers and legal guarantees, they differ from decentralization, devolution, and federal entities and form a sui generis type of territorial self-governance. The ontological closeness to federal units, which results from the characteristics of the second (strong self-rule) and third (guaranteed status) dimension, however, requires some closer inspection.[26]

Federal countries traditionally developed on the basis of a voluntary and constitutionally entrenched "agreement from below".[27] In contrast, territorial autonomies are usually no product of a bottom-up process and coming-together of entities to unite to a contractual foederatio but are granted top-down by "guarantees from above".[28] Apart from enumerated powers, most policy areas reside with the central government. Accordingly, territorial autonomies remain an integral part of the central state's legal system and are subject to all its national and international legal ties. In many cases, the laws passed by autonomy institutions require formal approval by the central government and can be rejected if they are incompatible with the national constitution or international treaties. As

[25] Keman, "Federalism and Policy Performance: A Conceptual and Empirical Inquiry."
[26] Suksi, *Sub-State Governance Through Territorial Autonomy: A Comparative Study in Constitutional Law of Powers, Procedures and Institutions.*
[27] Duchacek, *Comparative Federalism. The Territorial Dimension of Politics.*
[28] Schneckener, *Auswege aus dem Bürgerkrieg*, 335.

constituent units, federal regions participate on equal terms in the central legislative process via a second parliamentary chamber and approve laws affecting policy areas of the second tier, which includes, in particular, changes to the constitution. A supremacy clause, giving federal law precedence over sub-state law, serves to protect the unity of the state. As argued above, autonomy is based on the idea of distributing power away from the political center. Therefore, autonomous governments usually cannot veto national law-making, but are only involved if first-tier regulations affect the exclusive regulatory areas. This lack of decision-making authority at the central state level implies the protection of the central government's influence on regional policymaking, usually manifested by the absence of a supremacy clause.

An empirically useful conceptualization is ontologically broad enough to cover the whole range of territorial autonomies. Empirical studies that subsume territorial self-governance under umbrella terms such as territorial power sharing or regionalization run the risk of conceptual stretching and validation problems. In contrast, an overly high intension with too restrictive criteria, when, for example, definitions are enriched with normative elements such as social equality or liberal freedoms, leads to relevant cases being disregarded. The danger of too broad or too narrow autonomy definitions is particularly acute in cases of strong federal asymmetry in which both standard and non-standard types of territorial self-governance occur. Examples include India, Russia, or Spain, countries that are actually federal states, but in which not all sub-states are equipped with the same powers and certain regions on the second or even third tier fulfill the definition criteria of territorial autonomy. Based on the distinguishing features discussed above, a sub-state entity in this book is defined as a territorial autonomy if it is *a geographically defined area within a central state with a non-standard special status. This special status cannot be revoked unilaterally and includes exclusive executive and legislative powers.*

Identifying Cases of Post-conflict Territorial Autonomy

A historical review reveals dozens of autonomous territories, ranging from imperial cities of the Middle Ages to the dominions of the British Empire to Greek's Mount Athos. Apparently, not all territorial autonomies serve as managing institutions. Some territories were declared autonomous for economic reasons, such as Hong Kong in China or Sejong City in South Korea. Others, such as the Azores or Greenland are primarily functional autonomies, which have been granted self-governance for administrative reasons due to their geographical remoteness. These cases are of no particular interest to the present study.

The use of territorial self-governance as a conflict-regulating tool took place in three major waves, which do not occur coincidentally alongside the nationalist wave in the twentieth century, the emergence of powerful nation-states, and the resulting demands for self-determination by marginalized ethnic minorities. It was first the great geopolitical upheavals after the First World War and the flaring up of discourses on the right of peoples to self-determination that prompted various countries to turn away from the unitary nation-state principle and triggered a first wave of autonomy. The Saar region and the Åland islands, which both became autonomous territories under the aegis of the League of Nations or the Memel territory in present-day Lithuania, which was granted self-rule in 1924, prove to be excellent examples. After the Second World War, a second wave followed, creating autonomous regions such as South Tyrol in Italy and Denmark's Faroe Islands. While the European continent is the birthplace of conflict-regulating territorial self-government, the second wave of autonomy creations also spilled over to non-western countries, leading to the establishment of territorial autonomy to regulate ethnic tensions in India, Nicaragua, the Philippines, or Tanzania. Finally, the collapse of multiethnic empires and the resulting ethnic wars at the end of the Cold War led to a third and final wave, which brought about autonomous regions in Bosnia-Herzegovina, Georgia, or Moldova.

The investigation of the research question requires a systematic selection of relevant cases. Based on the identity-theoretical considerations discussed above, all ethnic groups enjoying substantial self-determination rights are selected in a first step. The comprehensive data of the Ethnic Power Relations project provide a suitable basis for this selection.[29] In a second step, it is analyzed whether these self-determination rights include territorial autonomy in the sense of the definition criteria set out above. The basis for the assessment is the legal status of the region in question as laid down in the respective domestic law, constitution, or peace agreement. All autonomy statutes which were implemented or fundamentally amended after 1945 and existed in at least a formal form until December 2016 are taken into consideration. Excluded from the analysis are interim

[29] Cederman, Wimmer, and Min, "Why Do Ethnic Groups Rebel?"; Vogt et al., "Integrating Data on Ethnicity, Geography, and Conflict."

autonomy solutions, such as South Sudan's Naivasha Agreement or the Fomboni Agreements for the Comorian island Anjouan. Such regulations do not intend to establish permanent power division on a territorial basis but constitute transitional solutions with other objectives. The analysis also excludes unilaterally declared autonomies, occupation zones, or de facto states like Western Sahara, Transnistria, or the Palestinian territories.

In order to exclude all non-conflict-regulating cases, a third step is to examine whether the respective autonomy was established as a result of an ethnic conflict. Whether this criterion applies is determined by using qualitative conflict data by the Heidelberg Conflict Barometer and the CONIS data set.[30] In contrast to other methods of conflict measurement, this approach also covers non-violent internal conflicts as well as information on conflict actors and conflict issues, which makes it possible to determine whether a conflict was actually an ethnic self-determination conflict. The case selection procedure leads to 19 cases of conflict-regulating territorial autonomy worldwide, established between 1922 and 2009 (Table 1.2).

The sample reveals a wide range of conflict-regulating autonomies. Most cases are located in Asia and Europe. In the Americas, Oceania, and on the African continent, the number of conflict-regulating autonomies is, despite the similar frequency of ethnic groups and self-determination conflicts, significantly lower. At first glance, no clear patterns can be detected with regard to structural or political conditions. The identified autonomous regions include island regions and mainland territories, sparsely populated areas, such as Guna Yala, with just about 15,000 inhabitants, as well as highly populous territories, such as Jammu and Kashmir or Catalonia with several million inhabitants. Territorial autonomies were implemented in ethnically homogeneous central states, such as Italy and Finland, but also in extremely heterogeneous countries, such as Papua New Guinea and Tanzania.

A similar high variance can be observed with regard to the democratic quality and economic performance of the central states, their government systems, or electoral regimes. The sample includes rich and consolidated liberal democracies (Finland or France), poor and defective democracies (Moldova or Tanzania) and hard autocracies (Iraq or Pakistan), parliamentary (United Kingdom), semi-presidential (France) and presidential

[30] Schwank, Trinn, and Wencker, "Der Heidelberger Ansatz der Konfliktdatenerfassung"; Trinn and Wencker, "Introducing the Heidelberg Approach to Conflict Research"; "Heidelberg Institute for International Conflict Research."

Table 1.2 Case selection

Case	*Abbrev.*	*Central state*	*Year*	*Conflict*	*Size (km^2)*	*Inhabitants*
Chittagong Hill Tracts	CHT	Bangladesh	1997	Limited War	13,300	1.5 Mio.
Åland	ALA	Finland	1922	Dispute	1,130	28,000
Corsica	COR	France	1992	Violent Crisis	8,720	3,38,700
New Caledonia	CAL	France	1998	Violent Crisis	18,600	2,13,600
Bodoland Territorial Area District	BOD	India	2003	Limited War	8,800	3.1 Mio.
Jammu and Kashmir	JAM	India	1947	War	1,01,400	12.6 Mio.
Nanggroe Aceh Darussalam	ACH	Indonesia	2006	War	55,400	5 Mio.
Kurdistan Region	KUR	Iraq	1970	War	48,900	5.3 Mio.
Trentino-Alto Adige/ Südtirol	TIR	Italy	1972	Violent Crisis	7,400	5,11,750
Autonomous Territorial Unit of Gagauzia	GAG	Moldova	1994	Dispute	1,800	1,60,700
Caribbean Coast Autonomous Region	ATL[a]	Nicaragua	1987	Violent Crisis	59,500	6,60,800
Gilgit-Baltistan	GIL	Pakistan	2009	Violent Crisis	72,900	1.3 Mio.
Comarca Guna Yala	GUN	Panama	1953	Crisis	2,340	15,541
Autonomous Region of Bougainville	BOU	Papua New Guinea	2002	Limited War	8,900	2,40,340
Autonomous Region in Muslim Mindanao	MIN	Philippines	1990	Limited War	11,600	3.7 Mio.
Autonomous Community Catalonia	CAT	Spain	1979	Dispute	32,000	7.5 Mio.
Basque Autonomous Community	BAS	Spain	1979	Violent Crisis	7,234	2.1 Mio.
Zanzibar	SAN	Tanzania	1963	Limited War	2,500	9,50,000
Northern Ireland	IRL	United Kingdom	1998	Limited War	13,800	1.8 Mio.

[a]Strictly speaking, the North Caribbean Coast Autonomous Region (RAAN) and the South Caribbean Coast Autonomous Region (RAAS) are two separate entities, but due to their identical institutional set-up, geographical proximity, common central state, conflict history, and political relations they are regarded as one case of territorial autonomy

systems (Nicaragua), states with majority voting systems (Bangladesh) as well as with proportional representation (Italy). A clearer picture emerges only with regard to conflict legacies: 84 percent of the sample's autonomy reforms were set up to settle a violent self-determination conflict, and in almost half of the cases tensions between ethnic groups escalated to a limited war or a war before implementation. Åland, Gagauzia, and Catalonia are the only cases of the sample where the establishment of the autonomy arrangement was preceded by a low-intensity, non-violent self-determination conflict.

Now that the conceptual foundations have been laid and the relevant cases selected, the next chapter deals with measuring the explanandum of the study, the consolidation status of conflict-regulating autonomies. The book then addresses its central research question, which has so far not been subjected to a systematic-comparative and case-oriented analysis in political science literature: which of the different settings under which territorial autonomies were established to regulate majority-minority conflicts have contributed to their consolidation? Which specific circumstances cause their failure?

Conclusion

Ethnic conflicts of self-determination are essentially conflicts over the recognition of cultural identity. The homogeneity claim of modern nation-states has turned many autochthonous groups into national minorities and, as Tilly puts it, has produced a "categorical inequality", which in many cases is highly conflictual.[31] The first chapter of this book has argued that peaceful coexistence between majority and minority in the aftermath of ethnic conflict often requires suitable institutional reforms. While minority rights are often too weak and, in many cases, neither the willingness to compromise nor the necessary overlapping identity is present for a functioning power sharing system, territorial autonomy is often a suitable option for "classical" minority conflicts. Differing from decentralization, devolution, and federalism, territorial autonomy was defined as asymmetric special status within a state which includes a high degree of self-rule as well as a status guarantee. The high performance potential of the managing institution, at least in theory, is based on the fact that through durable and guaranteed empowerment autonomy addresses the basic demands of

[31] Tilly, *Durable Inequality*, 172.

ethnic identity groups. It ensures official recognition and enables the (re-) creation of a positive group identity through far-reaching self-determination rights. At the same time, state sovereignty and territorial integrity are taken into account as the core concerns of a modern nation-state.

Although this potential is acknowledged by most authors, some critics argue that autonomy solutions allow elites to accumulate power, thereby promoting centrifugal activities and ethnic cleavages are strengthened rather than weakened. However, the ongoing academic debate about whether autonomy is a suitable option to regulate ethnic tensions is not a very fruitful one. There are both successful *and* failed cases. Obviously, autonomy consolidation is a strongly context-dependent phenomenon. As will be discussed in more detail in the following chapter, ethnic peace requires an ongoing process of mutual recognition between majority and minority. For such a process, autonomy reforms provide the appropriate institutional framework. At the same time, however, a set of specific necessary conditions is needed to initiate and sustain this social mechanism. If these conditions are not present, post-conflict autonomy reforms are doomed to failure.

References

Abushov, Kavus. "Autonomy as a Possible Solution to Self-Determination Disputes: Does It Really Work?" *International Journal on Minority and Group Rights* 22, no. 2 (2015): 182–201.

Åkermark, Sia Spiliopoulou. "Internal Self-Determination and the Role of Territorial Autonomy as a Tool for the Resolution of Ethno-Political Disputes." *International Journal on Minority and Group Rights* 20, no. 1 (2013): 5–25.

Anderson, Benedict R. *Imagined Communities: Reflections on the Origin and Spread of Nationalism*. New York: Verso, 2016.

Anderson, Liam, and Carlos Costa. "Survival of the Fittest: Explaining the Success of Ethnic Autonomy Arrangements." *Swiss Political Science Review* 22, no. 4 (2016): 516–544.

Armingeon, Klaus. "The Effects of Negotiation Democracy: A Comparative Analysis." *European Journal of Political Research* 41, no. 1 (2002): 81–105.

Cederman, Lars-Erik, Simon Hug, Andreas Schädel, and Julian Wucherpfennig. "Territorial Autonomy in the Shadow of Conflict: Too Little, Too Late?" *American Political Science Review* 109, no. 2 (2015): 354–370.

Daftary, Farimah. "Territorial Autonomy as a Response to Violent Self-Determination Conflicts: 'Too Little, Too Late'?" Paper for International Studies Association Annual Convention, San Francisco, 2008.

Danspeckgruber, Wolfgang. "Self-Governance plus Regional Integration: A Possible Solution to Self-Determination Conflicts." In *Autonomy, Self-Governance, and Conflict Resolution: Innovative Approaches to Institutional Design in Divided Societies*, edited by Stefan Wolff and Marc Weller. London: Taylor & Francis, 2005.

Dollard, John, Neal Miller, Leonard Doob, O.H. Mower, and Robert R. Sears. *Frustration and Aggression*. New Haven: Trubner & Company, 1939.

Duchacek, Ivo D. *Comparative Federalism. The Territorial Dimension of Politics.* Lanham: Rowman & Littlefield, 1987.

Forsberg, Erika. "Do Ethnic Dominoes Fall? Evaluating Domino Effects of Granting Territorial Concessions to Separatist Groups." *International Studies Quarterly* 57, no. 2 (2013): 329–340.

Gagnon, Alain, and Michael Keating, eds. *Political Autonomy and Divided Societies: Imagining Democratic Alternatives in Complex Settings.* New York: Palgrave Macmillan, 2012.

Ganguly, Rajat. *Autonomy and Ethnic Conflict in South and South-East Asia.* New York: Taylor & Francis, 2013.

Ghai, Yash. "Autonomy as a Strategy for Diffusing Conflict." In *International Conflict Resolution After the Cold War*, edited by Paul C. Stern and Daniel Druckman, 483–530. Washington, DC: National Academies Press, 2000.

Graham, Benjamin, Michael K. Miller, and Kaare W. Strøm. "Safeguarding Democracy: Powersharing and Democratic Survival." *American Political Science Review* 111, no. 4 (2017): 686–704.

Gurr, Ted Robert. *Why Men Rebel.* Princeton: Princeton University Press, 1970.

Hale, Henry E. "Divided We Stand: Institutional Sources of Ethnofederal State Survival and Collapse." *World Politics* 56, no. 2 (2004): 165–193.

Hartzell, Caroline A., and Matthew Hoddie. "Institutionalizing Peace: Power Sharing and Post-Civil War Conflict Management." *American Journal of Political Science* 47, no. 2 (2003): 318–332.

———. "The Art of the Possible: Power Sharing and Post-Civil War Democracy." *World Politics* 67, no. 1 (2015): 37–71.

Heidelberg Institute for International Conflict Research. "Conflict Barometer 2018." Heidelberg, 2019. https://hiik.de/conflict-barometer/.

Horowitz, Donald L. *A Democratic South Africa? Constitutional Engineering in a Divided Society.* Berkeley: University of California Press, 1991.

Keman, Hans. "Federalism and Policy Performance: A Conceptual and Empirical Inquiry." In *Federalism and Political Performance*, edited by Ute Wachendorfer-Schmidt. London: Routledge, 2000.

Kymlicka, Will. "Multiculturalism and Minority Rights: West and East." *Journal on Ethnopolitics and Minority Issues in Europe* 4 (2002): 1–26.

Lapidoth, Ruth. *Autonomy: Flexible Solutions to Ethnic Conflicts.* Washington, DC: United States Institute of Peace Press, 1997.

Lehmbruch, Gerhard. *Proporzdemokratie. Politisches System und Politische Kultur in der Schweiz und in Österreich*. Tübingen: J.C.B Mohr, 1967.

Lijphart, Arend. "Constitutional Choices for New Democracies." *Journal of Democracy* 2, no. 1 (1991): 72–84.

———. *Patterns of Democracy. Government Forms and Performance in Thirty-Six Countries*. New Haven and London: Yale University Press, 1999.

———. *The Politics of Accommodation. Pluralism and Democracy in the Netherlands*. Berkeley: University of California Press, 1968.

Mattes, Michaela, and Burcu Savun. "Fostering Peace After Civil War: Commitment Problems and Agreement Design." *International Studies Quarterly* 53, no. 3 (2009): 737–759.

Nordquist, Kjell-Åke. "Autonomy as a Conflict-Solving Mechanism—An Overview." In *Autonomy, Applications and Implications*, edited by Markku Suksi. Dordrecht: Kluwer Law International, 1998.

Norris, Pippa. *Driving Democracy. Do Power-Sharing Institutions Work?* Cambridge: Cambridge University Press, 2008.

Ottmann, M., and J. Vüllers. "The Power-Sharing Event Dataset (PSED): A New Dataset on the Promises and Practices of Power-Sharing in Post-Conflict Countries." *Conflict Management and Peace Science* 32, no. 3 (2015): 327–350.

Petersen, Roger Dale. *Understanding Ethnic Violence: Fear, Hatred, and Resentment in Twentieth-Century Eastern Europe*. Cambridge: Cambridge University Press, 2002.

Saideman, Stephen M. "Is Pandora's Box Half Empty or Half Full? The Limited Virulence of Secessionism and the Domestic Sources of Disintegration." In *The International Spread of Ethnic Conflict. Fear, Diffusion and Escalation*, edited by David A. Lake and Donald Rothchild, 127–150. Princeton: Princeton University Press, 1998.

Sambanis, Nicholas, Micha Germann, and Andreas Schädel. "SDM: A New Data Set on Self-Determination Movements with an Application to the Reputational Theory of Conflict." *Journal of Conflict Resolution* 62, no. 3 (2017): 656–686.

Schneckener, Ulrich. *Auswege aus dem Bürgerkrieg. Modelle zur Regulierung ethno-nationalistischer Konflikte in Europa*. Frankfurt am Main: Suhrkamp, 2002.

Schneckener, Ulrich, and Stefan Wolff. *Managing and Settling Ethnic Conflicts: Perspectives on Successes and Failures in Europe, Africa and Asia*. London: Hurst, 2004.

Schwank, Nicolas, Christoph Trinn, and Thomas Wencker. "Der Heidelberger Ansatz der Konfliktdatenerfassung." *Zeitschrift für Friedens- und Konfliktforschung* 2, no. 1 (2013): 32–63.

Siroky, David S., and John Cuffe. "Lost Autonomy, Nationalism and Separatism." *Comparative Political Studies* 48, no. 1 (2015): 3–34.

Sisk, Timothy D. "Electoral System Choice in South Africa: Implications for Intergroup Moderation." *Nationalism and Ethnic Politics* 1, no. 2 (1995): 178–204.

Spears, Ian S. "Africa. The Limits of Power-Sharing." *Journal of Democracy* 13, no. 3 (2002): 123–136.

Suksi, Markku. *Sub-State Governance Through Territorial Autonomy: A Comparative Study in Constitutional Law of Powers, Procedures and Institutions.* Berlin and Heidelberg: Springer, 2011.

Tilly, Charles. *Durable Inequality.* Berkeley: University of California Press, 1999.

Trinn, Christoph, and Thomas Wencker. "Introducing the Heidelberg Approach to Conflict Research." *European Political Science* 17, no. 1 (2016): 111–121.

Walsh, Dawn. *Territorial Self-Government as a Conflict Management Tool.* Cham: Springer, 2018.

Walter, Barbara F. *Reputation and Civil War: Why Separatist Conflicts Are So Violent.* Cambridge: Cambridge University Press, 2009.

Wimmer, Andreas. *Waves of War. Nationalism, State Formation, and Ethnic Exclusion in the Modern World.* Cambridge: Cambridge University Press, 2013.

Wolff, Stefan. "Conflict Management in Divided Societies: The Many Uses of Territorial Self-Governance." *International Journal on Minority and Group Rights* 20, no. 1 (2013): 27–50.

CHAPTER 2

Explaining Autonomy Success and Failure: An Identity-Based Approach

What makes post-conflict institutional reforms successful? Success and failure are notoriously difficult to measure scientific concepts. Nevertheless, it is widely agreed in literature that post-conflict institutions can be considered successful when tensions between rival parties no longer escalate into violent upheavals. A more ambitious understanding of success also includes the performance of institutions and the crisis resistance of established rules, for which the term consolidation is typically used. How can we empirically observe whether a conflict-regulating autonomy has consolidated or not?

Generally speaking, post-conflict institutional consolidation is based on two intertwined premises: on the one hand, institutional longevity and crisis robustness, and, on the other, the continuous fulfillment of certain functions expected by the institutional framework. In order to be considered a credible and predictable structure for interactions between majority and minority, autonomy institutions must survive on a permanent basis. On the other hand, the expected function of autonomy reforms is fulfilled when ethnic conflicts within the autonomous territory do not re-escalate, but rather are managed and processed on the basis of the formalized rules of the established framework. A consolidated autonomy system is seen by both the titular nation and the minority as the best available and most beneficial option for achieving their key interests. This presupposes, as the next section argues, that attitudes and behavior have changed accordingly, so that the majority and minority can both consider themselves as

F. Schulte, *Peace through Self-Determination*, Federalism and Internal Conflicts,
https://doi.org/10.1007/978-3-030-37587-4_2

constitutive parts of a demos. In contrast, autonomy reforms are considered to have failed if these two interrelated premises are not or not fully met and at least one actor resorts to a strategy of violence.

Measuring Autonomy Success and Failure

These two premises of functionality and stableness can be empirically captured using three indicators. First, and most importantly, consolidated autonomies are characterized by the absence of a violent conflict on the autonomous territory after the implementation of the special status (*peace*). Second, autonomy institutions have been in force de jure without any interruption since their introduction. At best, they have survived several changes of government at the state and sub-state levels without the autonomy rights being curtailed (*durability*). Third, there is at least a fundamental acceptance of the autonomy solution by group representatives, politicians, and parties, who express this in positive statements on multiculturalism in speeches, declarations, or party programs. In contrast, large secessionist movements and mobilization attempts on the one side and re-centralization efforts or repressive assimilation measures on the other side indicate that the managing institution is not met with general approval (*acceptance*).

On basis of the three criteria, I create four qualitative anchors of the outcome: successful autonomy (value 1), partly successful autonomy (values 0.8–0.67), partly failed autonomy (value 0.33), and failed autonomy (values 0.2–0). To determine the variable values, the entire period from the adoption of the respective autonomy statute to the end of 2018 is observed.[1] Cases are considered completely successful if all three criteria are met unequivocally. This applies to five cases of the sample, namely Åland, Gagauzia, Guna Yala, New Caledonia, and South Tyrol. An autonomy arrangement is considered to be partially successful if the conflict seems to be peacefully regulated, but one or both of the two other criteria is not fully met. This applies to Aceh, the Basque Country, Bougainville, Catalonia, and Corsica.

Territorial autonomy is considered a partial failure if ethnic tensions in the autonomous area no longer escalate, but the autonomy institutions neither show a sufficient lifespan nor are generally accepted. Empirically,

[1] Chapter 3 provides a more detailed overview as well as robustness tests of the calibration of the outcome condition.

however, it can be observed more frequently that although the criteria of duration and acceptance are met, there are still occasional violent clashes between insurgents and state forces. In this case, too, an autonomy arrangement is considered as partially failed according to the aforementioned assumptions. The prerequisite is then, however, that the conflict has not intensified. This applies to three cases in the sample, Kurdistan, Northern Ireland, and Zanzibar. An autonomy is regarded as a complete failure if the self-determination conflict could not be ended or has even intensified. The two other criteria are of lesser importance in these cases. If one of those is met, the case is coded with 0.2. The autonomies of the Atlantic region, Bodoland, Chittagong Hill Tracts, Gilgit-Baltistan, Jammu and Kashmir, and Mindanao are hence failed cases of post-conflict autonomy reforms (Table 2.1).

The number of successful (10) and failed cases (9) of territorial self-government is balanced. This first finding confirms the variance in consolidation outcomes of post-conflict autonomy reforms and underlines the initial assumption that territorial autonomy is neither a panacea nor inevitably doomed to failure. This variance needs to be explained.

Table 2.1 Autonomy success and failure

	Peace	*Durability*	*Acceptance*	*Outcome*	*Score*
ALA	(+)	(+)	(+)	Successful	1.0
CAL	(+)	(+)	(+)	Successful	1.0
TIR	(+)	(+)	(+)	Successful	1.0
GAG	(+)	(+)	(+)	Successful	1.0
GUN	(+)	(+)	(+)	Successful	1.0
CAT	(+)	(o)	(o)	Partly successful	0.8
BAS	(+)	(+)	(o)	Partly successful	0.8
COR	(+)	(+)	(o)	Partly successful	0.67
ACH	(+)	(+)	(o)	Partly successful	0.67
BOU	(+)	(+)	(o)	Partly successful	0.67
KUR	(o)	(+)	(o)	Partly failed	0.33
IRL	(o)	(+)	(o)	Partly failed	0.33
SAN	(o)	(+)	(o)	Partly failed	0.33
BOD	(−)	(o)	(o)	Failed	0.22
ATL	(−)	(o)	(o)	Failed	0.22
CHT	(−)	(−)	(−)	Failed	0
JAM	(−)	(−)	(−)	Failed	0
GIL	(−)	(−)	(−)	Failed	0
MIN	(−)	(−)	(−)	Failed	0

It is noticeable that all fully successful cases are relatively small and rather sparsely populated, remote regions. The largest territorial autonomies in the sample are all classified as failed cases. On average, the area of failed cases is more than twice as much as that of successful cases. Remarkable is also the small number of inhabitants of the successful autonomies compared to the high number of residents of failed autonomies. Small regions, like Åland, Gagauzia, or Guna Yala are easier to control and easier to govern. They need fewer financial resources and have limited human and power-political resources for mobilization. Their survival chances as independent territories are comparatively low (Fig. 2.1).

It becomes also apparent that most successful autonomies are in fact located in liberal European democracies, which are economically highly developed, stable, and not affected by negative diffusion effects of bad neighborhoods. It also seems that autonomy consolidation depends heavily on the previous intensity of the ethnic conflict. While in Åland or Gagauzia the conflict intensity was at a very low level, other cases such as Mindanao or Jammu and Kashmir were affected by bloody ethnic wars.

At first glance, these initial findings are hardly surprising. There is little doubt in conflict research that democratic rule, state capacity, economic development, and low conflict intensity increase the *probability* of peaceful conflict resolution. Democracies offer alternative and peaceful ways of dealing with political conflicts and advocate tolerant, liberal, and thus

Fig. 2.1 Map of successful and failed autonomies. (*Source*: Own illustration. For presentation purposes, the central states and not the autonomous regions are color-coded. Darker colors denote more successful cases)

peaceful values. Economically strong central states can afford institutional reforms, can manage to contain secessionist efforts by making financial concessions to poorer regions, and can mitigate prevailing grievances between ethnic groups through welfare programs. Low conflict intensity eases reconciliation between ethnic groups and makes peace more likely.

However, a closer look at the consolidation outcomes reveals dozens of deviant cases. Catalonia or Aceh, for example, are large and populous territories and are considered at least partly successful. Northern Ireland, which has been classified as partly failed due to ongoing ethnic tensions, is located in a rich, highly developed, and democratic central state. In contrast, more successful autonomies are located in poor, underdeveloped, and highly defective democracies such as Moldova and Panama. Spain's autonomous regions are at the same level of consolidation as Aceh in Indonesia or Bougainville in Papua New Guinea.

In contrast to previous assumptions in autonomy research, it seems that the "classical" peace factors such as the quality of liberal democracy, the level of state capacity, and economic performance alone cannot satisfactorily explain the differences in consolidation outcomes. While these variables are likely to have a positive effect on ethnic peace, it remains unclear whether they are also causally necessary for autonomy success. But it is the minimum conditions that must be unraveled in order to determine which factors are sufficient for post-conflict autonomy reforms to be successful. In other words, what should peacemakers primarily focus on?

A comprehensive explanation of this variance first requires a systematic and theory-bound selection of success factors, a thorough explanation of why exactly these conditions are pivotal, and a causal argument of why these are interrelated necessary conditions. To this end, the study turns to the micro level, toward cultural identity groups and interethnic behavior, to understand the basic prerequisite for ethnic peace—ethnic recognition.

Understanding Ethnic Recognition

Humans are social beings and automatically belong to a variety of social collectives. Such social groups have common goals and unite individuals on the basis of an at least rudimentary we-consciousness, which determines who belongs to the group and who does not. While some collectives, such as sport clubs or art societies are only one and short-lived collective among many, others are primary groups—dominant and durable collectives in the life of its members. Besides the family and close relatives, also ethnic groups belong to this category of primary groups. These social collectives are usually indispensable for their members because they are emotionally and permanently bound to the group. Being a member of them is a matter of belonging, not of achievement. In other words, such groups create *identity*.

A major part of the individual self-concept stems from belonging to collectives and is social identity. This belonging is anchored intrapsychically and is, as many psychologists have shown in experiments, a basic human need.[2] Personal self-description does not work without the self-allocation to social groups, which presupposes that individuals find some commonalities that distinguish them from others. Sherif, Tajfel, and others have shown that minimal, often trivial commonalities are sufficient to build social groups, create in-group favoritism, and foster competitive behavior toward out-groups.[3] What is decisive for the group constitution is not whether the commonalities actually exist or whether they are objectively important, but *Gemeinschaftsglauben*—the belief in belonging together and the assertion of equality accepted by all members of the social collective.[4]

Identity is a specific and changeable relationship between people and themselves and their social environment which needs to be produced and continuously re-produced through social interactions and communication processes. The element that perfectly enables enduring communication and reproduction, while developing sufficient daily-life relevance for group members, is culture. Culture is a symbolic and meaningful framework of orientation and the dominant social element that creates and preserves social identity. In this book, social collectives with a social identity based on cultural elements are defined as *ethnic groups*.

The constitutive elements of culture are language and symbols, tradition and customs, religion, and historical narratives. Language names and interprets reality and is perpetuated communication which makes the existence of an identity group not being tied to the limited lifespan of its members. Traditions are a form of socially learned behavior which provide orientation and also help to overcome temporality. Religion offers believers a complete interpretation of the world, gives orientation, and reduces

[2] Sherif and Sherif, Social Psychology; Brewer, "In-Group Bias in the Minimal Intergroup Situation"; Burton, Conflict.

[3] Tajfel, "Social Categorization"; Tajfel, *Human Groups and Social Categories.*

[4] Weber, *Wirtschaft und Gesellschaft. Grundriss der Verstehenden Soziologie.*

complexity even in transcendence. History, too, has a cross-generational stabilization function. The shared story, glories and traumas, and the myth of a common descent create a strong sense of community.

Social Identity Theory (SIT), one of the grand theories in psychology, argues that social identity not only defines group membership, but also evaluates this membership.[5] The self consists of a descriptive component, the self-concept, and an evaluative component, self-esteem. People generally strive for a high self-esteem and a "positive" identity.[6] They want to be perceived as being good, competent, and decent. Since the self is also based on belonging to social collectives, it is of exceptional importance which status the in-groups have in comparison to out-groups. To assess their own status, people are constantly comparing themselves to others.[7] When people make social comparisons between their own group and an out-group, they want their in-group to be positively evaluated by relevant out-groups. A positive social identity results from "won" comparisons between the in-group and out-groups, whereas the goal of the differentiation process is to achieve or maintain superiority. The "prize" of this competition is the achieved social status of the group. The lower the subjective status of a group compared to other relevant groups, the lower the "contribution" to the social identity of the group members and to their self-esteem. In other words, people want to be recognized by others as members of a social group that is important to them, since their self-esteem depends on this membership and the status of the group. The stronger the identification of the individual with a social collective is, the greater the need for recognition.

While hardly present in the research field of ethnic politics so far, the concept of recognition can be found in various philosophical and social scientific works from Kant to Honneth or Taylor. Although used in different contexts and often replaced by synonyms such as "dignity" (Hegel), "Positionsgut" (Frank), or "Tymos" (Fukuyama), recognition usually implies the general acceptance of individuals or collectives, mutual respect and, to some extent, appreciation by others.[8] In the context of ethnic identity groups, the desire for recognition inevitably refers to the cultural

[5] Tajfel and Turner, "An Integrative Theory of Intergroup Conflict"; Tajfel and Turner, "The Social Identity Theory of Intergroup Behaviour."

[6] William, *The Principles of Psychology*; Burton, *Violence Explained.*

[7] Festinger, "A Theory of Social Comparison Processes."

[8] Frank, *Choosing the Right Pond*; Fukuyama, Identity.

elements mentioned above. Recognition is present if groups reciprocally accept that members of an out-group differ in regard to their language, religion, or customs but do not devalue them because of these perceived differences. However, recognition is not a fixed and irreversible state of intergroup relationship, but a social process that must be initiated and constantly maintained.

SIT posits that intergroup comparisons are effectively a struggle over the relative status of one's in-group. Group members are highly motivated to protect and enhance the positivity of their group in order to protect and enhance their own personal self-esteem. People whose group is threatened by out-groups develop more in-group identification and are more likely to derogate out-group members to maintain and protect the positivity of their identity.[9] Superior groups fight to protect their status and lower status groups struggle to lose their stigma. Such social comparison processes are especially emotional for the members of ethnic groups as the status, prestige, and social valence of the group is *directly* attached to the group members lives on basis of life-determining cultural elements such as language or religion.

It is important to note that identity threats do not make out-groups enemies per se. For an ethnic conflict to actually arise, groups need to consider their situation to be changeable in principle and no other strategies are available for group members to respond to threats other than competition with other groups such as leaving the group or compensate for negative feedback on an alternative domain.[10] In addition, the group must perceive the current group status as being unfair. It is the discrepancy between what is desired and what has been achieved, relative deprivation, that causes frustration that can easily be instrumentalized by leaders for group mobilization and collective action.[11]

An ethnic group comes to recognize that inequalities exists, so the group understands that not all groups in society experience deprivation and superior groups enjoy what they lack. This is followed by the generation of feelings among the group members that the current group status is inequitable and can be rectified only through collective action. Political, economic, social, and cultural asymmetries between the in-group and the

[9] Sanderson, Social Psychology, 338.

[10] Lemaine, "Différenciation Sociale et Originalité Sociale"; Cadinu and Cerchioni, "Compensatory Biases after Ingroup Threat."

[11] Gurr, *Why Men Rebel.*

out-group are transformed into grievances. The perception of grievances in turn strengthens the we-feeling. "Ethnic conflict is", as Horowitz states, "at bottom, a matter of comparison".[12] As mentioned earlier, it is not just relatively deprived groups that find their status unfair and take action to create a positive group status. The maintenance or protection of the status of relatively privileged groups such as Catalans in Spain or Slovenes in the former Yugoslavia can also lead to ethnic tensions. Collective violence is not the inherent goal of martial tribes, but rather a last-option strategy for achieving the basic need of identity recognition. The causal chain from relative deprivation to grievances to domestic conflict cannot be explained without the instrumentalization of feelings associated with identity threats. It must be articulated who is responsible for the unfair status. The evoked fantasies, fears, and frustrations are applied to both the current situation and the identified out-group. A rebel group also needs the opportunity to rebel and the resources to do so like personnel, financial resources, and military equipment. When it comes to group organization, identity groups have a considerable advantage over other actors. Group identity is a "powerful mobilizing agent", as the social glue that holds the group together already exists and is extremely strong.[13]

The individual has an enormous personal interest in restoring or maintaining group status. The defeat of one's own group inevitably means the devaluation of one's own culture, one's own identity, and the rule of the victorious out-group. Thus, collective action problems are comparatively easy to overcome. Ethnic conflicts are not primarily based on incompatible political interests—that is, what the conflicting parties want, or say they want, but what they are, or believe they are. The recourse on the socio-psychological of intergroup behavior helps to identify the normative point of orientation for successful ethnic conflict regulation: Ethnic group members cannot be persuaded to simply abandon the satisfaction of their basic need for recognition. Regardless of resources or power, groups will agitate, although in different ways, for the satisfaction of this human need.

In principle, ethnic recognition can be achieved in different ways. While in some cases multicultural policies, protective minority rights or even symbolic recognition may be sufficient to ease intergroup tensions, severe cultural cleavages and escalated conflicts between groups require potent institutional reforms. Institutions can reduce uncertainties, promote

[12] Horowitz, *Ethnic Groups in Conflict*, 197.
[13] Stewart, *Horizontal Inequalities: A Neglected Dimension of Development*, 5:3.

bargaining, constrain political rule, and, consequently, embed cultural conflict in non-violent borders. For asymmetric majority-minority conflicts, as argued above, territorial self-governance arrangements are a particularly relevant option for institutional peacebuilding. While from a theoretical point of view, they offer a high potential for the re-organization of intergroup relations in multicultural postwar societies due to the guaranteed special status and a substantial degree of self-rule, their consolidation is shaped significantly by various contextual conditions that enable or hinder ethnic recognition and, consequently, ethnic peace.

So far, the literature lacks a comprehensive theoretical synthesis between institutionalist and structuralist explanations of ethnic peace, and the basic socio-psychological assumptions on intergroup behavior described above. Such a theoretical synthesis, however, as presented in the following section, is a highly fruitful undertaking and provides a comprehensive explanation for the success and failure of post-conflict institutional reforms.

A Multi-causal Model of Autonomy Success and Failure

Three basic assumptions can be derived from the previous remarks. First, ethnic groups have a comparatively high need for recognition of their social identity. While ethnic conflicts generally result from the non-recognition of ethnic diversity, ethnic peace is in fact a state of mutual recognition between cultural identity groups. Ethnic recognition needs to be understood as a social process that must be initiated and continuously maintained. Second, when it comes to post-conflict institutional design, territorial autonomy arrangements provide a suitable framework for ethnic recognition due to their inherent power-dividing logic and guaranteed empowerment. Third, the consolidation of post-conflict autonomy reforms is obviously a highly context-dependent phenomenon. Some exogenous factors seem to work for a process of mutual recognition while others seem to prevent it. In order to fully explain the success and failure of territorial autonomy systems, these three basic assumptions must be set in a causal relationship.

As described above, the consolidation of autonomy presupposes, on the one hand, that the autonomous institutions remain in place on a permanent basis. This necessitates the fundamental acceptance of the institutional compromise by all relevant actors. On the other hand, the institutional arrangement must continuously fulfill its specific function, which is achieved when conflicts between majority and minority within the autonomous territory do not re-escalate, but rather are managed on the basis of formalized and acknowledged rules. In contrast, territorial autonomy as a managing institution is considered to have failed if these premises are not or not fully met and at least one actor resorts to a strategy of violence. A consolidated autonomy is considered by both the titular nation and the minority as the best possible option. Attitudes and behavior have changed accordingly so that out-groups are generally accepted as constitutive parts of the demos.

Although mutual recognition, as understood here, does not imply solidarity, amicable feelings, or admiration, its realization in the context of ethnic conflicts is anything but an easy task. In a simplified sense, ethnic recognition in post-conflict situations can be understood as a three-stage social process: the *acceptance* of institutional reforms as new rules of the game must be followed by *cooperation* efforts at the elite level, which in turn are a prerequisite for deeper *rapprochement* and reconciliation processes at the societal level. The core of this book's argument is that the reaching of these levels depends not solely on the chosen institutional arrangement but hinges decisively on a specific set of conditioning exogenous factors, enabling and fostering *acceptance*, *cooperation*, and *rapprochement*. This theoretical framework, as described in detail below, helps to explain the high variance of consolidation outcomes and gives an in-depth explanation why some autonomy solutions have worked while others have disastrously failed in weakening ethnic rivalries.

Despite the high importance of social collectives and intergroup behavior, ethnic elites, politicians, or leaders of secession movements play a pivotal role in ethnic self-determination conflicts. They act as strategic agenda-setters and mobilizers and their political strategy gives significant impulses to their followers. However, ethnic self-determination conflicts are not purely top-down, elite-driven struggles for power, as instrumentalist or primordialist approaches assume. For their political survival, ethnic leaders need the backing of ordinary group members. Both are expected to share the primary interest in empowerment and official recognition, whereas elites act as agents of general group interests.

The first precondition for ethnic recognition is that autonomy reforms are broadly accepted as the new rules of the game by all ethnic elite fractions. When do elites accept that the ethnic settlement area remains part of the central state and that transferred competencies provide for self-governance, not full independence? Ethnic elites take a positive view on institutional reforms if these credibly promise permanent and far-reaching empowerment and, consequently, political power for them. The chances of reaching concessions on self-determination using alternative strategies are deemed lower and more costly.

Assuming an essentially strategic and vote-seeking behavior, ethnic leaders are expected to accept and support institutional reforms if this decision is backed and rewarded by their followers. Ordinary group members, for their part, are positive about institutional reforms if they expect them to improve their personal situation. This depends in the case of ethnic group members, as outlined above, decisively on the relative group status. Destructive actions are omitted if group members have credible reasons to believe that self-determination rights and cultural protection will endure in the long term. There must be a credible commitment by the central government that territorial autonomy will improve the minority's group status and that majority dominance and cultural exclusion will not prevail in the future. The fundamental acceptance of autonomy reforms by the minority group is the first necessary step toward autonomy consolidation. However, in praxis, it is a fragile approval that can quickly vanish and be overwhelmed by hate speeches of radical wings, polarizing sentiments, and recriminations. Reciprocal recognition presupposes, as a sequential step, the gradual intensification of cooperation efforts between the central government and ethnic leaders.

A region's autonomous status alone does not break the deep cultural cleavages between rival groups and the diametrical positions they have on political and cultural self-determination, state sovereignty, and political dominance. The initial acceptance of institutional compromises can only be transformed into a continuous and crisis-resistant support if both parties have access to suitable cooperation forums. Following consociationalist assumptions, it is adequate opportunities for long-term cooperation that allow conflict parties to move away from extreme demands, to find compromises, and to foster political rapprochement as a second necessary step of mutual recognition.

These cooperation forums, however, do not have to be designed as grand coalitions or forms of executive power sharing but exist alongside the vertical distribution of power. Therefore, the existence and functionality of the managing institution does not *entirely* depend on effective interethnic political bargaining and compromising behavior. However, inclusive institutions enhance the chances of a conflict-dampening balance of power, reduce the likelihood of centrifugal activities, and make autonomy solutions to fully work in practice. Territorial self-government means neither independence nor segregation and political isolation. In practice, bureaucratic regulations between state tiers must be drawn up, financing issues clarified, and unregulated areas of competence defined, which necessitates a considerable degree of cooperation between regional and central state level. Cooperation efforts in conflict-laden contexts are considered particularly promising if actors have some incentives and face sufficient pressures to continue the cooperation and to adhere to the agreed rules of the game. In addition to suitable cooperation opportunities, this is the second important basic prerequisite for successful elite cooperation as a subsequent step of the recognition process.

As argued above, ethnic peace requires mutual recognition on a broad societal basis. In order to bridge the gap between rulers and ruled, I again follow basic consociational assumptions and assume that perpetuating processes of cooperation and rapprochement at the elite level will gradually shift to cooperation at the mass level. Ongoing cooperation efforts signal not only that both sides take the autonomy reform project seriously, but also that the other side can be perceived as a trustworthy actor. If interethnic cohabitation becomes the chosen route, this makes centrifugal activities become the less promising option.

As many case studies have shown, rapprochement and reconciliation processes at the societal level require certain political drivers, which are usually to be found in civil society or social movements. But also businesses and the private sector, which have little interest in growth-inhibiting cultural cleavages, can play an important role in this respect. This third and final phase is expected to be the longest and most difficult, as old stereotypes, prejudices, and mistrust must be dismantled. But if it is successful, multiculturalism as a political culture of ethnic diversity has developed in which majority and minority recognize each other as culturally different ethnic groups, but do not devalue each other on the basis of cultural differences. This forms the basis for the consolidation of conflict-regulating territorial autonomy.

This theoretical framework also provides a comprehensive explanation for autonomy failure. Post-conflict autonomy reforms fail to regulate ethnic self-determination conflicts, if this three-stage mechanism is not initiated or interrupted. Radical elite factions do not support the compromise solution but return to their maximal demands of separatism or full sovereignty. This is to be expected when leaders see no credible guarantee for real self-determination and political power as promised competencies are not transferred or commitments are not adhered to. If the political and cultural hegemony of the central state persists, ordinary group members consider the institutional reforms as appeasement strategy by the majority group, which does not address their real needs of identity protection and status improvement. Perceived identity threats result, as has been outlined above, in further countermeasures, which are taken to establish a positive group identity. Grievances are easily instrumentalized by ethnic demagogues for further mobilization and collective action.

Based on the theoretical assumptions, the three-stage process of recognition serves as the underlying mechanism at the micro level between autonomy implementation and its consolidation outcome. Considering institutional success as a highly context-sensitive phenomenon, post-conflict autonomy reforms fail when favorable conditions are absent or even disruptive factors occur. The two theoretical models developed can be illustrated in Figs. 2.2 and 2.3.

Now that the theoretical basis has been laid, the next theoretical step is now to identify core variables that are potentially causally relevant for the postulated factor chain. From a theoretical point of view, any chosen condition must have a positive effect on the acceptance of autonomy reforms, elite cooperation, or social rapprochement as the three decisive stages of ethnic recognition. If these conditions are not or not fully met in the consolidation period, autonomy failure and ongoing separatist conflict should be observable. It must then apply empirically that the conditions are individually necessary and together sufficient to explain the respective

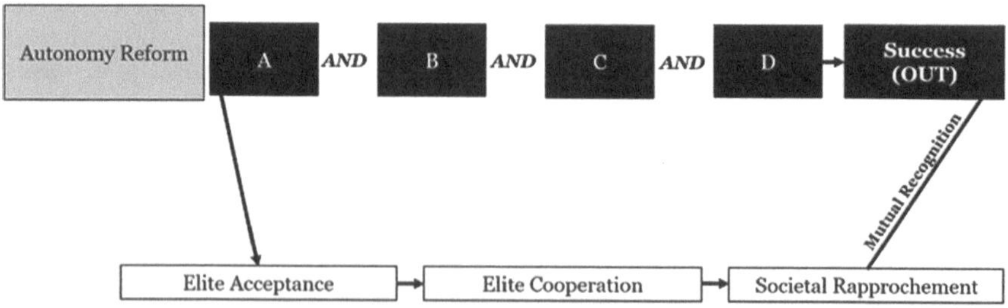

Fig. 2.2 Theoretical model of autonomy success. (*Note*: The uppercase letters describe the presence of favorable conditions in a consolidation phase. *Source*: Own illustration)

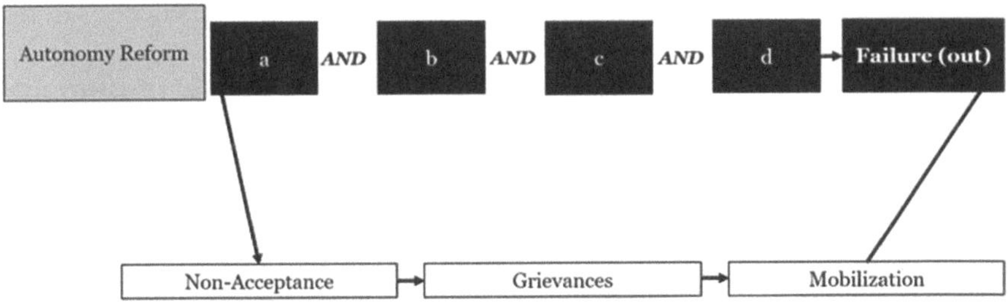

Fig. 2.3 Theoretical model of autonomy failure. (*Note*: The lowercase letters denote the absence of favorable conditions in a consolidation phase. *Source*: Own illustration)

consolidation outcome. Finally, it must hold true that relevant conditions actually affect the postulated mechanisms.

Identifying Favorable and Unfavorable Conditions

The sheer number of conditions that have been discussed and included as independent variables in qualitative or quantitative studies already indicates that institutional success as a highly complex empirical phenomenon cannot be fully explained by individual structural or actor-centered factors.

Although positive effects can be expected from several structural variables, which we can empirically observe at least to some extent, not all of these variables seem to be causally relevant. Besides providing convincing comprehensive theoretical explanations, autonomy research lacks robust empirical findings in this regard. If there are any, they are mostly based on case study evidence that can hardly be generalized. The best example is the largely uncontested consensus in literature of a "democracy requirement". However, post-conflict institutional reforms are most often needed in non-democratic contexts, which, in turn, means that at least some territorial autonomies must have survived in regimes that were less than optimally democratic when the institutional arrangement was implemented.

We find successful cases in flawed, rather unstable, and poor democracies, regions that combine regional autonomy with local power sharing and some that work without this feature. While some autonomies contain mediation instances or international guarantees others do not. This makes the presumption that these prominent success factors alone are decisive quite problematic. Apparently, not individual factors, but rather a specific combination of several factors contributes to autonomy success. This combination needs to be unraveled.

It is also not very intuitive to focus only on structural or institutional variables that largely disregard the actor level that is, as outlined above, so important in ethnic conflicts. On the other hand, purely actor-based approaches lack convincing explanations as to why groups or group leaders behave in a certain way and what encourages or constrains their actions. Both logics of explanation must therefore be harmonized in a meaningful way. This study addresses these shortcomings of existing research on territorial self-government and takes into account a carefully selected set of conditions, both actor-centered and structural at the macro as well as the micro level.

The ethnic conflict, in particular its intensity and the specific claims made by the ethnic self-determination movement, for which I use the generic term *conflict strategy*, is an ex ante success factor and of paramount importance for the activation of the recognition-mechanism. If mere demands for autonomy have been made, elites will find it less difficult to accept and support autonomy as a managing institution. If this goal was largely pursued by peaceful means, there is a good chance that elites will be able to reach agreement on implementation, adhere to negotiated deals, and engage in cooperation processes. However, if the strategy involved secessionist claims, then autonomy is only a second choice that does not meet the ultimate goal of independence. If the group also pursued a violent strategy, which was answered by the central government with the same means, a process of rapprochement between the groups is much harder to achieve.

The acceptance of elites and group members hinges, as mentioned, on a credible guarantee of official recognition and empowerment. This depends crucially on how far the transferred autonomy rights extend. The more regulatory areas the regional government and hence the ethnic group can decide on, the greater the "contribution" to a positive group identity and the less likely are destructive measures to restore a positive group identity. The *scope of autonomy* thus plays a vital role for the success of an autonomy system.

Contrastingly, persistent *horizontal inequalities* between majority and minority are diametrically opposed to a broad popular acceptance of post-conflict institutional reforms. Adapting the growing body of evidence finding that multidimensional group inequalities fuel grievances and enhance the likelihood of ethnic mobilization, this book argues that political empowerment alone will not prevent a group from taking centrifugal activities if economic or social inequalities persist in a consolidation phase.

The quality of liberal *democracy* also has, as is generally assumed, a positive effect on the consolidation of an autonomy system. Democratic regimes itself operate as a rule-based system for processing and managing political conflicts. Democratic regimes only create the conditions for rapprochement processes at the political level by granting liberal freedoms, participation rights, and offering cooperation opportunities.

As already mentioned, cooperation at elite level also requires external incentives, pressures, and monitoring. Another success factor of post-conflict autonomy reforms is their *internationalization*. This includes both the international engagement and the international integration of the subnational region itself. International organizations serve as important mediators and watchdogs in the event of renewed tensions in a consolidation phase. The integration of autonomous regions into international or regional networks provides further communication channels and offers a kind of "external" recognition.

Conflict Strategy

What political strategy did the group or an organization acting on behalf of the group pursue to achieve self-determination and ethnic recognition? With the concept of strategy, I am referring to a longer-term orientation toward a specific goal, which also has an instrumental dimension. For the consolidation of an autonomy system, it is not trivial, whether rights of self-determination were demanded almost peaceful or whether a bloody war was raging over the separation of a territory. The behavior of rebelling ethnic groups is inherently determined by the unfulfilled need for a positive group identity and by no means a pure rational action. Nevertheless, it is, as mentioned above, not free of strategic considerations, but rather is a very serious and emotional game of moves and counter moves. Ethnic leaders choose the strategy that promises the greatest opportunity to achieve self-government and cultural recognition and usually prioritize less costly non-violent strategies.

Social movements that articulate their goals peacefully, whether conventionally through elections, party work, or lobbying, or unconventionally but non-violently, through protest marches or strikes, are more likely to receive concessions than using violent strategies. About 40 percent of all peaceful self-determination movements achieve at least some of their goals, while 80 percent of all violent movements make no progress at all.[14] Apparently, the greatest chance for institutional consolidation exists when the ethnic group has reached a special autonomy status for their settlement area non-violently through demonstrations, mass rallies, or protest marches. In contrast, the slightest chance of autonomy success exists when ethnic leaders chose a violent strategy to achieve the goal of full independence.

In the case of previous demands for autonomy, the strategic objective and the outcome achieved are coherent. The implemented managing institution corresponds to the initial strategy goal of the elites, which makes broad acceptance of institutional reforms appear likely. Re-emerging conflicts between the regional and the central government revolve around the concrete institutional set-up, the division of competencies, or financing issues, but not around the kind of institutional recipe. In the case of preceding secession claims, territorial autonomy as a compromise solution is only a second choice and does not correspond to the actual goal of ethnic leaders. It is then very likely that radical wings will regard this as a defeat and use the empowerment to raise new secessionist demands.

Just as important as the articulated goals are the specific actions of ethnic movements to achieve self-determination. If groups are systematically excluded from gaining political influence, conventional opportunities for political influence are not, or at least not fully, available. If non-violent demonstrations are suppressed, group elites are arbitrarily arrested, and repressions conducted, group members may choose the path of violence as a last resort. However, violent strategies always imply high costs as they provoke repressive reactions by the central government, which aims at maintaining its sovereignty and deterring other groups from seeking secession in the future. Through violent actions, the group has challenged the state's legitimacy and monopoly on the use of force, which leads to plausible doubts as to whether this will be respected once the group has received political empowerment. If this leads the central state not to fully implement or even to revoke the autonomy agreement, this means a renewed loss of status for an ethnic group and considerably increases the probability of a renewed conflict escalation.[15]

When the group has pursued a primarily peaceful strategy and expressed its willingness to compromise in negotiations, it is seen by the central

[14] Chenoweth and Lewis, "Unpacking Nonviolent Campaigns."

[15] Siroky and Cuffe, "Lost Autonomy, Nationalism and Separatism."

government, the public, and external actors as a reliable and trustworthy actor who does not abuse its empowerment. This facilitates the building of cooperation and bargaining efforts among elites, which, according to the postulated mechanism, should contribute to the success of autonomy reforms. Almost all self-determination movements try to positively influence public opinion beyond state borders. Although violent protests usually achieve greater media attention, peaceful protests generate more support and have some moral advantage. In contrast, a violent conflict strategy divides the social collective into those who are willing to fight and those who cannot or do not want to fight. Since it is easier to mobilize people to attend a mass rally than to ask them to take a gun or grenade in their hands, a peaceful self-determination movement can rely on broader support from various sections of the population. If the autonomy goal is achieved through the participation of many, broad acceptance of the institutional reforms at the mass level as an important prerequisite of autonomy consolidation is a likely outcome. In the case of too extreme demands and excessively cruel violence, undecided sections of the population may side with the central government, whose repressive countermeasures are seen as justified and as guaranteeing stability, security, and development. The assumptions can be summed up with the following hypothesis:

H1 A peaceful, non-secessionist conflict strategy is a necessary condition for the success of a conflict-regulating territorial autonomy.

Scope of Autonomy

As argued above, institutional reforms will be broadly accepted and supported if they credibly promise permanent and far-reaching political empowerment. The more policy areas the group can decide upon, the greater is the "contribution" to a positive group identity. A high scope of autonomy fulfills the goal of official cultural recognition and far-reaching self-determination. If the scope of transferred powers is too narrow, a group will not be able to decide upon its own cultural and political affairs. Group members then oppose institutional reforms as pseudo-empowerment and appeasement strategy by the central government that does not address their real needs. Since this maintains the perceived identity threat, radical wings can easily mobilize for further secessionist protests and countermeasures.

A major trigger for many conflicts within autonomous regions—and empirical challenge for scientists as well—is the often large gap between the de jure regional authority defined in legal documents and the actual level of self-determination a group enjoys. Since there is no "contribution" to a positive identity through competencies that exist only on paper, both the de jure and the de facto scope of autonomy must be taken into account. Only if group members can speak their respective languages in everyday life, practice their religions, and use their own symbols without any restrictions, will territorial self-governance lead to ethnic recognition and fulfill its intended conflict-regulating purpose. Six policy dimensions appear to be of particular importance for assessing the scope of self-rule in ethnic contexts: (1) cultural dimension; (2) security dimension, (3) fiscal dimension, (4) social dimension, (5) international dimension, and (6) constitutional safeguarding dimension.

As ethnic conflicts are cultural conflicts, (1) sufficient cultural competencies are the backbone of successful conflict regulation through ethnic empowerment. On basis of the theoretical assumptions made, it can be concluded that comprehensive cultural competencies should cover language and religion legislature, the right to education in the groups' own language, the right to set up cultural organizations, as well as the right to use own symbols, such as flags, stamps, or anthems.

In the aftermath of ethnic conflict, the guarantee of (2) internal security is a key issue. While the central government is by definition responsible for ensuring external security, a strong regional government can command regional police forces and is able to maintain public order and protect its inhabitants from criminal acts. Furthermore, the judiciary plays a crucial role for internal security. Since autonomies are most often subject to the legal system of the state, they generally do not have their own local courts. If there is no parallel traditional jurisdiction within the autonomous territory, it is crucial for this dimension whether the inhabitants have free access to the state courts.

A high degree of autonomy presupposes (3) financial powers and the possibility of freely deciding how the financial resources are used. Sufficient financial resources are a fundamental prerequisite for taking action in other policy areas and, consequently, for real self-determination. A strong regional government has budgetary rights, can independently tax its population, and can borrow additional funds without authorization.

Furthermore, self-government presupposes that those who are meant to govern themselves are able to do so and are not hindered by poverty, lack of health, or education. It is (4) socio-political competencies that create the prerequisites for real empowerment by protecting group members from elementary human risks and creating a certain degree of social security. A well-functioning health and education system managed by the regional administration is crucial for this dimension.

In a globalized world, even sub-state actors must articulate their interests on the global stage in order to be heard. Thus, (5) international competencies complete the policy spectrum. This dimension includes the right to conclude international contracts as well as to join or form international or regional organizations. Powerful regional governments must agree and can veto if an international agreement concluded by the central government affects exclusive regional competencies. Decisive is, as mentioned above, not only the scope of transferred competencies but also the guarantee that these self-determination rights can be exercised on a permanent basis. Therefore, I include (6) safeguarding as an additional dimension in the concept of autonomy scope.

While the autonomy status cannot be reversed by definition, strong autonomies are protected by some additional "stability anchors." The special status is entrenched in the state constitution, whereby amendments require the approval of the sub-state government or regional assembly. Furthermore, a powerful autonomy arrangement contains mediation authorities, such as commissions with equal representation, arbitration tribunals, or an ombudsperson. These bodies can mediate in cases of conflict between the state tiers and avoid the upsurge of tension. They offer the group an additional guarantee that the central government is serious about the empowerment and its continued existence.

A high scope of autonomy includes comprehensive rights to these six dimensions, which can also be exercised de facto. This allows, according to the theoretical expectations, a broad popular acceptance and support for the institutional reforms as a first step of the three-stage mechanism.

H2 A high scope of autonomy is a necessary condition for the success of a conflict-regulating territorial autonomy.

Horizontal Inequalities

Tocqueville already notes that "almost all the revolutions that have changed the face of peoples have been made in order to consecrate or to destroy inequality".[16] While many scholars confirm this positive correlation, others have rejected inequality as an explanatory variable for

[16] Tocqueville, "Über Die Demokratie in Amerika," 462.

explaining domestic conflicts.[17] This empirical inconsistency results largely from the inaccurate response to the question between whom and on what dimension social asymmetries exist.

Inequality may be present among individuals, vertical inequality, or between social collectives, so-called horizontal inequality. Both types are not necessarily congruent, as high horizontal inequality can exist in a society with low vertical income inequality if low incomes are generated by one social group and higher incomes by another. In ethnic contexts, horizontal inequalities are present when members of a specific cultural identity group are politically, economically, socially, or culturally significantly worse or better off than other relevant groups in the country, in particular the majority population. Building on Stewart's pioneering work, numerous empirical studies find that the horizontal type of inequality indeed increases the probability of intrastate conflict.[18] This has some important implications for ethnic conflict regulation.

Asymmetries between groups, as argued above, are a dominant source of grievances. If, in the course of relative deprivation processes, the status of the in-group is perceived as unfair, feelings of envy, resentment, and anger arise. Non-recognition as the core of the ethnic conflict is basically the perception of horizontal inequalities. As each individual has a high personal interest in restoring or protecting the in-group status, collective action problems can easily be overcome. It is hard to imagine that group members are not aware of the relative status of their ethnic group. But the group status is probably overrated or underestimated. A group that is only slightly discriminated against may perceive disadvantages being more serious and harmful than they actually are. However, it will hardly rate its status as better than that of a privileged group. In other words, the perception of inequality is fundamentally based on the actual situation of a social group. However, the specific extent and sources of inequality might be very banal for outsiders.

Research has shown that it is rather irrelevant whether grievances and perceived identity threats are based on political, economic, cultural, or social group asymmetries.[19] Different dimensions of inequality often occur

[17] Fearon and Laitin, "Ethnicity, Insurgency and Civil War"; Collier, Hoeffler, and Rohner, "Beyond Greed and Grievance. Feasibility and Civil War."

[18] Stewart, *Horizontal Inequalities and Conflict. Understanding Group Violence in Multiethnic Societies*; Østby, "Polarization, Horizontal Inequalities and Violent Civil Conflict"; Cederman, Gleditsch, and Buhaug, *Inequality, Grievances, and Civil War.*

[19] Rørbæk, "Killing in the Name of …?"

simultaneously, as, for example, a lack of education (social dimension) is strongly correlated with low monetary income (economic dimension) which may lead to political apathy (political dimension) and so on. This leads to the assumption that political empowerment alone is not sufficient for building peace if, at the same time, strong economic or social inequalities between the majority and the minority persist in a consolidation phase. In other words, whereas territorial self-governance provides for a certain degree of political and cultural equality through the transfer of autonomy rights, its consolidation depends on whether economic or social inequalities between the respective groups persist, which tend to create new conflict-fueling grievances.

H3a The absence of strong economic inequalities between the group with autonomy status and other relevant groups in the country is a necessary condition for the success of a conflict-regulating territorial autonomy.

H3b The absence of strong social inequalities between the group with autonomy status and other relevant groups in the country is a necessary condition for the success of a conflict-regulating territorial autonomy.

These hypotheses, however, presuppose that all inequality dimensions actually increase the likelihood of the occurrence of ethnic conflict. If the existence of a specific inequality dimension makes the occurrence of ethnic conflict more likely, it is to be expected that its persistence in the consolidation phase will in turn hinder peaceful conflict regulation, as groups do not see any improvement in their status and thus continue to fight for a positive group identity. To test this underlying presumption, I analyze the political, economic, social, and cultural status of all relevant ethnic groups worldwide between 2000 and 2009.[20] The pre-analysis reveals that roughly half of all ethnic groups worldwide are politically discriminated against. Around 40 percent are considered economically disadvantaged. At the social level, 36.6 percent are discriminated against, compared to 28.5 percent at the cultural level. Of the groups in the sample, 18.9 percent are disadvantaged in all four dimensions. As expected, ethnic groups often experience inequalities on multiple dimensions (Tables 2.2 and 2.3).

[20] See Appendix for details on operationalization and coding decisions.

Table 2.2 Frequency of occurrence of horizontal inequalities, 2000–2009

Inequality dimension	*Political*	*Economic*	*Social*	*Cultural*
Discriminated against (%)	51.5	39.9	36.6	28.5
Not-discriminated against (%)	48.5	60.1	63.4	71.5

Table 2.3 Simultaneous occurrence of horizontal inequalities, 2000–2009

Inequality dimension	*Political (%)*	*Economic (%)*	*Social (%)*
Economic	31.6	–	–
Social	28.9	32.0	–
Cultural	23.4	24.2	24.0

While these numbers shed light on the high relevance of ethnic marginalization and majority dominance, a logistic regression analysis confirms that all inequality dimensions are indeed conflict relevant. The existence of political, cultural, but also economic and social inequalities between groups significantly increases the likelihood of an outbreak of domestic conflict. This applies to all intensity levels, with the exception of full discrimination for the likelihood of the occurrence of disputes, crises, and violent crises. In line with other grievance-based research, we can expect that groups experiencing strong discrimination on all dimensions tend to resignation and apathy rather than to antagonism and collective action. This in turn lowers the risk of political conflict (Table 2.4).

Most political science literature so far focuses on the political or economic exclusion of groups to explain ethnic rebellion. Forms of social or cultural marginalization have often been overlooked, in particular in large-n quantitative studies. However, horizontal inequality is apparently a multidimensional and interdependent social phenomenon, whereas all inequality dimensions produce conflict-fueling grievances. This, in turn, means that the consolidation of autonomy as a form of political empowerment and cultural protection presupposes the absence of strong social and economic inequalities between majority and minority. Only if there are no strong grievances present in a consolidation phase can the process of mutual recognition be initiated. In contrast, the persistence of social and economic inequalities leads to ongoing struggles of an ethnic groups for a positive in-group status and, consequently, to autonomy failure.

Table 2.4 Horizontal inequalities and conflict probability, 2000–2009

Reference: no conflict	*Coeff.*	*Sign.*	*Odds ratio*	*Reference: no conflict*	*Coeff.*	*Sign.*	*Odds ratio*
Dispute				*Violence crisis*			
POL	0.261	0.269	1.298	POL	1.157	0	3.182
ECON	0.459	0.138	1.583	ECON	0.088	0.61	1.092
SOC	0.237	0.462	1.267	SOC	1.252	0	3.498
CULT	0.776	0.008	2.172	CULT	0.697	0	2.009
Total	−0.146	0.659	0.864	Total	−0.56	0.004	0.571
Crisis				*(Limited) war*			
POL	0.15	0.404	1.162	POL	0.327	0.275	1.387
ECON	0.672	0.003	1.957	ECON	0.877	0.016	2.404
SOC	1.259	0	3.524	SOC	1.985	0	7.281
CULT	0.337	0.127	1.400	CULT	−0.349	0.38	0.706
Total	−0.704	0.005	0.495	Total	0.46	0.273	1.584

Democracy

The institutional consequence of guaranteeing individual and collective self-determination is democratic rule. The concept of territorial autonomy entails the inherently democratic idea that a particular demos can regulate its own affairs without any authorization. Democratic rule presupposes self-determined and participating citizens, whereas, ensuring individual self-determination requires sufficient participation and freedom rights—that is, democratic structures. The concepts of democracy and autonomy are obviously intertwined, as has been most clearly elaborated by consociational democracy theory.[21] From a peace research perspective, democracies are, despite being systems of contestation and organized uncertainty, able to manage and process political conflicts on the basis of established and accepted rules and legitimized negotiation mechanisms. Already Rousseau and Kant drew attention to the internally and externally peace-promoting effect of democratic regimes as institutionalized rule systems for social conflict management. The correlation between peace and democracy has since been confirmed by generations of scholars. This prominent finding as well as the theoretical embedding of the concept of "cultural autonomy" in consociationalism as a democracy theory made many autonomy

[21] Schmidt, *Demokratietheorien. Eine Einführung*; Lehmbruch, *Proporzdemokratie. Politisches System und Politische Kultur in der Schweiz und in Österreich*; Lijphart, "Consociational Democracy."

researchers conclude that territorial self-governance as a managing institution requires a thoroughly liberal democratic breeding ground to unfold its positive effects on majority-minority relations.[22]

Only a political regime that is itself inherently based on the idea of self-determination and that has manifested this principle through political rights and civil liberties will credibly grant autonomy to ethnic minorities. Only if political action is bound to accepted and normative rules based on fair competition and human rights can the division of power be successful in the long term as upcoming conflicts between the local level and the central level are regulated on the basis of established mechanisms. Furthermore, democratic rule creates various opportunities for bargaining and cooperation on the political level within governments, parliaments, or parties. Such cooperation opportunities are, as has been argued above, decisive for rapprochement processes among political elites as the second necessary step of ethnic recognition.

Surprisingly, the democracy-requirement argument has hardly been tested in literature and needs some specification when regarding autonomy as a managing institution for the regulation of ethnic self-determination conflicts. While ethnic conflicts occur in both democracies and non-democracies, they are longer-lasting and have a higher risk to escalate in autocratic regimes. Autonomy solutions are, therefore, not exclusively, but to a larger extent, needed in non-democratic environments. Keeping up the argument implies that many of today's successful cases must have survived in central states that were less than optimally democratic when the institutional reforms were set up, but which did become more democratic in the reform consolidation phase.

However, if the central state is not already a full liberal democracy, which is usually the case in post-conflict situations, we should observe that during the implementation of sub-state reforms, opportunities for cooperation are created and developed by enabling fair competition and inclusive decision-making processes on central state level. The breeding ground of participation rights and civil liberties must at least steadily grow in order to enable continuing bargaining efforts and make actors to move away

[22] Lapidoth, Autonomy. Flexible Solutions to Ethnic Conflicts; Nordquist, "Autonomy as a Conflict-Solving Mechanism-an Overview"; Ghai, *Autonomy and Ethnicity. Negotiating Competing Claims in Multi-Ethnic States*; Åkermark, "Internal Self-Determination and the Role of Territorial Autonomy as a Tool for the Resolution of Ethno-Political Disputes."

from the conflict-laden zero-sum game. The democracy-hypothesis must consequently be extended to include the process of democratization:

H4 A democratic or democratizing central state is a necessary condition for the success of a conflict-regulating autonomy.

However, the argumentation then faces a serious dilemma, since democracy and democratization are by no means congruent when it comes to peace as dependent variable. Paradoxically, while fully-fledged democracies are associated with peaceful conflict management, the road toward peace and democracy is rocky. War-to-democracy processes entail particular risks that enhance the probability of renewed fighting and endanger post-conflict institutional reforms. Whereas consolidated democracies are able to manage internal disputes peacefully through social participation, established regulatory mechanisms, and regular opportunities to replace the government, strong autocracies resort to the use of repressive means, powerful ideologies, or cooptation of challengers to overcome incompatibilities. Highly defective democracies or weak autocracies are often incapable of either of these methods, which in turn increases the potential for domestic conflicts. This phenomenon also applies to the likelihood of violent ethnic conflicts.[23]

Democratization entails the de-privileging of former authoritarian rulers and opens the political arena. This creates considerable polarization in multiethnic post-conflict societies, as group boundaries rather than similarities are emphasized when competing for votes and offices. Each electoral competition provides new incentives for the use of force by those who lose, or fear losing, power and by those who feel that they should gain more political influence. In young democracies, often neither a civic culture, nor stable and effective state institutions which would be able to steer the competition for offices into peaceful channels are existent. In order to maintain the democracy argument, it must be theoretically feasible to assume that post-conflict autonomy reforms can mitigate the major risk of democratization in multiethnic states, that is, the ethnicization of political competition and conflict re-escalation.

Executive power sharing is based on the very idea that the best way to ensure peace and democracy is to bring elites from warring cultural or

[23] Sambanis, "Do Ethnic and Nonethnic Civil Wars Have the Same Causes? A Theoretical and Empirical Inquiry"; Reynal-Querol, "Ethnicity, Political Systems, and Civil Wars."

social groups into a jointly-run governing coalition. However, as argued above, such arrangements face some serious challenges on the ground, as sharing power legitimizes and equips former belligerents with political power and prevents a vibrant and alternating democratic opposition. Furthermore, consociations often do not allow for the effective participation of social groups not aligned with the constituent groups, which is contrary to the idea of democratic rule. By giving all major players a stake in decision-making processes, competition is shifted "inward" which easily leads to instability and political deadlocks that can endanger both democracy and peace.

Territorial autonomies, in contrast, are primarily based on the principle of power-division. As an ethnic minority receives territorial self-governance and is to a large extent excluded from central decision-making processes, there is neither the dilemma of which groups to include in a grand coalition nor a considerable high risk of dangerous blockades. Rival groups do not have to compromise on every single political decision, but are both spatially and institutionally separated, which largely prevents inefficiency as the Achilles' heel of executive power sharing. Power-dividing thus may even have an efficiency advantage that has a positive effect on democratization. The faster state capacity and bureaucratic effectiveness are rebuilt in a post-conflict environment, the better for democratization and the rule of law. A rapid establishment of regional authorities and the fast provision of state services may also have a positive impact on the popular acceptance of institutional reforms. Reforms, as has been argued, are accepted whenever people can expect their personal situation to improve.

Above all, however, autonomy reforms increase the political importance of the second state tier. This defuses competition for political power and positions of influence as a major threat of post-conflict democratization. An additional level of political authority with exclusive law-making powers makes an ethnic group's struggle for control of the political center simply becoming less important. Research finds indeed evidence that strong group cohesion in combination with regional empowerment enhances people's willingness to participate in elections on subnational level.[24] This strengthens the legitimization of the political system which in turn is conducive to stable democratic governance. Granting territorial self-government means that not everything is at stake in national elections

[24] Schrijver, Regionalism After Regionalisation; Henderson and McEwen, "A Comparative Analysis of Voter Turnout in Regional Elections."

for minorities since the electoral game is no longer an all-or-nothing decision about which group can rule over which. This mitigates the zero-sum character of politics. The implementation of a territorial autonomy creates a vertical separation of power and prevents an excessive concentration of power and the hegemony of a dominant group.

Nevertheless, autonomy and vertical power-division do not mean political isolation. Democratization creates a number of ties with the central state level, for example through local parliamentarians, joint governmental bodies, courts, or regional political parties. Despite the division of powers, these ensure the exchange of information and the permanent cooperation between the central government and the regional government.

Internationalization

In many cases in the past, self-determination groups have sought the political or financial support of external players such as kin states or diaspora groups. We also frequently observe diffusion from within to outside when self-determination movements have negative spill-over effects in neighboring states. An ethnic conflict is considered internationalized only when the international community tries to end it. As will be outlined below, the international level is a fundamental part of a comprehensive explanation of the consolidation of a conflict-regulating autonomy system. I use the term "internationalization" as a generic term that comprises two separate conditions that play a role at different times in the consolidation phase: On the one hand, the participation of international organizations in the negotiations on a region's autonomy status, and on the other hand, the integration of the autonomous region into international or regional organizations at a later date.

Involvement of International Organizations

Given the zero-sum nature of ethnic conflicts, it seems unlikely that groups who deeply distrust each other will be able to find a way out of this security dilemma by themselves and rearrange their social relationships without any external help. Conflict parties must be convinced of the mutual benefits of institutional reforms and persuaded to engage in cooperation and bargaining. As argued above, mutual recognition requires not only adequate opportunities to cooperate, but also the support of external actors to actually do so and to adhere to agreements.

While third countries, most notably patronage states, might take sides with their ethnic kin or allies and thereby exacerbate rather than reduce rivalries, international organizations enjoy a higher degree of moral authority and may use their wide range of conflict resolution tools to break conflict dynamics and reduce conflict intensity to a more manageable level. International organizations can play an important mediating role in the relationship between the central government and ethnic leaders. International mediation is not based on the use of direct violence and does not aim to help a party win, but rather tries to change perceptions through incentives and political or economic pressure. Despite some cases of blatant failure, research finds robust evidence for the positive effects of international mediation efforts on peace processes. Empirical data from the Civil War Mediation Dataset (CWM) suggests that only about a quarter of all mediation efforts are completely unsuccessful.[25]

However, unlike other studies in the field, this book does not focus on the role that international organizations play in achieving post-conflict reform agreements, but primarily on the long-term impact of international mediation on institutional consolidation. An international organization involved in the peace negotiations between the conflict parties on the establishment of territorial self-government will also monitor the development of the reforms, supervise compliance with the established provisions, and intervene in cases of emerging tensions. Such activities are expected not only for organizations such as the United Nations, but also for regional international organizations whose member states may themselves be most affected by the negative effects of a conflict due to their geographical proximity or trade relations. In some cases, international engagement may include sending special envoys or even peacekeeping troops to prevent a renewed outbreak of ethnic violence.

The monitoring by international organizations hinders the central government from re-centralizing powers and abolishing a region's special status at the earliest opportunity. At the same time, it effectively counteracts emerging secession claims. Besides sharp swords, such as resolutions or economic sanctions by the member states, international involvement also has a positive effect on the consolidation process through the softer instrument of publicity. The participation of international organizations puts the peace process on the international agenda, informs an organization's member states and the public about treaty violations or outrageous crimes that jeopardize the reputation, diplomatic and economic relations of the

[25] DeRouen, Bercovitch, and Pospieszna, "Introducing the Civil Wars Mediation (CWM) Dataset."

central state, and diminish support for ethnic self-determination. Ethnic leaders recognize that their statements and actions are constantly under observation, that the chances of unilateral declarations of independence being internationally acknowledged are low, and that territorial self-government is the optimum achievable. International involvement thus dampens extreme demands and has a positive effect on the acceptance of institutional reforms.

In addition to fostering the process of mutual recognition through monitoring and escalation prevention, also international organizations provide important forums for the exchange of information between the conflicting parties within their structures or support such bottom-up reconciliation initiatives by civil society organizations or the private sector. Bureaucratic assistance, donor conferences, or regular diplomatic roundtables enable the conflict parties to get into contact with each other in a secure environment. This prevents the emergence of dangerous security dilemmas, reduces fears, and forms the basis for deeper cooperation at political level.

H5a The engagement of international organizations in reform negotiations is a necessary condition for the success of a conflict-regulating territorial autonomy.

International Integration

As important as the engagement of international organizations may be, it usually ends after a certain period of time, as involvements have limited mandate and financial and human resources. Mediations, for example, last about 126 days on average.[26] In such a short time span, no managing institution can consolidate, let alone fundamentally change the conflictual relationship between majority and minority. Building peace is usually a long and stony path, which may take decades and often entails huge challenges, such as spoiler groups, economic crises, or bad neighborhoods that can lead to the failure of the peace process. Hate speeches by ethnic demagogues or rallies by radical forces can open old wounds and lead to a new re-ethnicization and polarization of politics. In order to avoid dangerous setbacks and to prevent an interruption in the process of mutual recognition, short-term participation by international organizations is not sufficient for autonomy consolidation. Ethnic groups need continuous support

[26] Own calculations based on the CWM dataset.

from external actors in order to transform a conflictual relationship into a peaceful co-existence.

Such permanent support can take place via international integration, that is, the political integration of the sub-state entity itself into international networks. The specific type of the organization and its objective seems to be of secondary importance, as long as the regional government as representative of the autonomous region, and not of the central state, is a participating member of the international network. Of particular importance are regional organizations or sub-state cooperation networks which, due to the geographical proximity of their members, have good knowledge of the involved actors, the conflict history as well as cultural or even personal peculiarities. It is to be expected that integration into international organizations is usually a success factor at a later stage, as membership already presupposes a certain lifespan and thus a certain degree of institutional consolidation. In the long term, however, the second condition of internationalization is of vital importance for the process of mutual recognition, as it facilitates ongoing cooperation at the political level. International organizations are rule-based and manifested forms of cooperation between their members. Organizational membership implies an easy access to permanent communication channels and cooperation opportunities through which critical information can be exchanged. The continuous exchange of information within a reliable and predictable negotiating framework with established procedural rules further reduces uncertainties, creates security of expectation, and enables mutual recognition.

While a positive effect on deeper political cooperation as the second important step of the postulated mechanism presupposes that both the central government and the regional government are members of the same organization, it also appears beneficial if the autonomous region is a member of networks other than the central state. When the subnational region is included in international networks, it is officially recognized as an autonomous and special minority region by other international actors. In a way, the special status manifests itself, which is a further guarantee for a group that their territorial self-government will endure in the future. This may be an important and less costly alternative option to demands for more self-determination rights or even independence. At the same time, organizations are a permanent contact forum, as other members can easily be made aware of violations of the rules of self-determination and can mediate in the event of tensions within the organizational structures.

Secessionist demands, on the one hand, and efforts to re-centralize regional powers on the other, inevitably attract the attention of the international community. This encourages cooperative and compromising behavior on both sides.

H5b International integration is a necessary condition for the success of a conflict-regulating territorial autonomy.

Conclusion

Unlike previous research efforts in the field, this book does not aim to explain why parties agree on autonomy reforms or why conflict-regulating territorial self-governance generally works or not. In contrast, the study provides a comprehensive explanation for the unresolved question why some autonomies have consolidated in post-conflict contexts while others have not significantly reduced ethnic tensions. From an empirical point, autonomies as a managing institution can be considered consolidated when no violent conflict prevails on the autonomous territory, regional institutions have reached a certain lifespan and, most importantly, all relevant actors accept the autonomy solution as the new rules of the game.

The application of these criteria illustrates the considerable variance in the consolidation outcomes of the 19 cases of the sample. As assumed in recent literature, a majority of post-conflict territorial autonomies was indeed set up to regulate low-intensity self-determination conflicts in rich and industrialized democracies. However, the many deviant cases clearly indicate that obviously not all of the independent variables discussed in existing literature are also causally relevant to explain autonomy success and failure. Partial evidence of the positive effect of single variables such as economic development, a clear division of competencies between state tiers, international or domestic legal guarantees is not sufficient to fully explain this complex phenomenon. Rather, a combination of certain exogenous factors seems to be at work in consolidation periods.

A thorough understanding of autonomy consolidation requires a close look on ethnic peace as the normative endpoint of post-conflict institutional engineering. Drawing on Social Identity Theory allows us to analyze intergroup behavior and to understand the core of ethnic peace, a state of mutual recognition between majority and minority. The chapter emphasized that ethnic groups have a considerable high need for recognition because their we-feeling is primarily based on life-determining cultural elements such as language or religion. Recognition is achieved, when majority and minority groups perceive themselves as culturally diverse, but despite these differences see each other as constitutive parts of the demos. From a theoretical point of view, autonomy systems are capable of facilitating this process of ethnic recognition, even in the context of highly polarized self-determination conflicts.

However, ethnic recognition does not fall from the sky, but presupposes three intermediate steps, namely the initial acceptance of reforms, continuing elite cooperation, and rapprochement processes at the societal level. Complementing purely institutionalist and structuralist approaches, this chapter has argued that this three-stage social mechanism does not occur in a vacuum, but rather depends on various conditioning variables that provide a fertile breeding ground for autonomy consolidation. Whereas most studies so far have focused on single independent variables, this study expects a fruitful combination of structural and actor-centered factors at the micro and macro level to produce a specific consolidation outcome.

A high degree of self-determination promises regional elites influence and political power and, consequently, increases the willingness to accept autonomy reforms. Despite a political and cultural empowerment through territorial self-governance arrangements, economic or social grievances can lead to further polarization. A high degree of equality between the majority population and the group with special status will therefore have a positive effect on the success of conflict-regulating autonomy. While a low prior conflict intensity and a lack of demands for full independence are expected to be beneficial for rapprochement and reconciliation processes, adequate cooperation arenas are required to ensure long-term majority-minority cooperation. Since post-conflict autonomy reforms in most cases are not accompanied by a high degree of liberal democracy, the consolidation of autonomy requires at least a continuous deepening of democratic qualities. Democratization is expected to be less conflict-prone, as autonomy reforms weaken the struggle for control of the political center.

The involvement of international organizations in peace talks increases the chance that actors will continue cooperation efforts and political rapprochement. However, since international engagement is usually of limited duration, it is necessary to successively embed autonomous regions in policy networks that provide further communication channels and represent a form of "external" recognition. From a theoretical point of view, these factors have a decisive impact on the three stages of ethnic recognition and thus provide a sufficient explanation for autonomy success.

Conversely, following the theoretical considerations, we should empirically observe that failed cases of autonomy reforms were established in the aftermath of highly violent secessionist wars without the participation of an international organization and are equipped with a relatively low degree of self-rule. In these cases, it is expected that strong economic and social inequalities between majority and minority persist in the post-conflict period and produce new grievances. It is also expected that failed cases are hardly integrated into international or regional networks and are found primarily in autocracies or heavily defective democracies. From an empirical point of view, the next step is now to measure these variables and to determine whether these conditions really constitute a minimum set of necessary conditions for autonomy success.

Appendix

Horizontal Inequalities

POL_HU and CUL_HU are expected to be no longer present in consolidation phases, as they are, at least de jure, abolished with the establishment of territorial self-government as a managing institution. However, both inequality dimensions are considered here in order to conduct a complete test of the interdependency and multidimensionality of intergroup asymmetries. The following indicators are used to operationalize the four dimensions (Table 2.5).

From an empirical point of view, inequality implies a significant deviation from the national average on the respective dimension. The independent variables are coded dichotomously (discriminated against/not-discriminated against) on group-year level on the basis of the respective indicators for all relevant groups in all states with more than 500,000 inhabitants. The dataset consists of 1209 ethnic groups in 156 countries.

A group is relevant if its interests are represented by at least one actor in the national political arena, or if members of the group are systematically discriminated against.[27] All titular nations are coded as "not-discriminated against". In most cases, only one indicator per dimension is

[27] Cederman, Min, and Wimmer, "Ethnic Politics and Armed Conflict: A Configurational Analysis of a New Global Data Set."

Table 2.5 Indicators for inequality dimensions

Inequality dimension	*Indicators*
Political (POL_HU)	Access to political power
Economic (ECON_HU)	Income, Assets
Social (SOC_HU)	Unrestricted access to education and health facilities; citizenship
Cultural (CUL_HU)	Unrestricted practice of Language, Religion, Traditions

taken into account. For example, if a significantly lower enrollment rate indicates social inequality, the group´s health status is not further reviewed. The dependent variable for the regression analysis is the conflict intensity variable of the Heidelberg conflict approach.[28]

For the political dimension, data from the EPR dataset is used.[29] Politically excluded are groups without executive influence opportunities (powerless) and those who are discriminated against (discriminated). The economic, social, and cultural dimension is coded on the basis of qualitative data from the World Directory of Minorities and Indigenous Peoples, the International Work Group on Indigenous Affairs, the United Nations as well as the NGO Saferworld.[30] In addition, data for the economic and cultural dimension are synchronized with the Minorities at Risk (MAR) and the All Minorities at Risk (AMAR) datasets.[31] A dummy variable for cultural inequality is coded on the basis of the MAR variables CULPO1 (restrictions on the exercise of a religion) and CULPO2 (restrictions on the exercise of a language) and the value labels "informally restricted", "somewhat restricted", and "sharply restricted".

[28] HIIK, "Heidelberg Institute for International Conflict Research."

[29] Cederman, Wimmer, and Min, "Why Do Ethnic Groups Rebel?"

[30] Minority Rights Group International, "World Directory of Minorities and Indigenous Peoples"; IWGIA, "International Work Group for Indigenous Affairs"; UNHCR, "Refworld"; Saferworld, "Saferworld."

[31] Minorities at Risk Project, "Minorities at Risk"; CIDCM, "Minorities at Risk (MAR) Codebook Version"; Birnir et al., "Socially Relevant Ethnic Groups, Ethnic Structure, and AMAR."

References

Åkermark, Sia Spiliopoulou. "Internal Self-Determination and the Role of Territorial Autonomy as a Tool for the Resolution of Ethno-Political Disputes." *International Journal on Minority and Group Rights* 20, no. 1 (2013): 5–25.

Birnir, J. K., J. Wilkenfeld, J. D. Fearon, D. D. Laitin, T. R. Gurr, D. Brancati, S. M. Saideman, A. Pate, and A. S. Hultquist. "Socially Relevant Ethnic Groups, Ethnic Structure, and AMAR." *Journal of Peace Research* 52, no. 1 (2015): 110–115.

Brewer, Marilynn B. "In-Group Bias in the Minimal Intergroup Situation: A Cognitive-Motivational Analysis." *Psychological Bulletin* 86, no. 2 (1979): 307–324.

Burton, John, ed. *Conflict: Human Needs Theory.* London: Palgrave Macmillan, 1990.

Burton, John Wear. *Violence Explained: The Sources of Conflict, Violence and Crime and Their Prevention.* Manchester: Manchester University Press, 1997.

Cadinu, Maria Rosaria, and Marcella Cerchioni. "Compensatory Biases After Ingroup Threat? Yeah, But We Have a Good Personality?" *European Journal of Social Psychology* 31, no. 4 (2001): 353–367.

Cederman, Lars-Erik, Kristian Skrede Gleditsch, and Halvard Buhaug. *Inequality, Grievances, and Civil War.* Cambridge: Cambridge University Press, 2013.

Cederman, Lars-Erik, Brian Min, and Andreas Wimmer. "Ethnic Politics and Armed Conflict: A Configurational Analysis of a New Global Data Set." *American Sociological Review* 74, no. 2 (2009): 316–337.

Cederman, Lars-Erik, Andreas Wimmer, and Brian Min. "Why Do Ethnic Groups Rebel? New Data and Analysis." *World Politics* 62, no. 1 (2010): 87–119.

Chenoweth, Erica, and Orion A. Lewis. "Unpacking Nonviolent Campaigns: Introducing the NAVCO 2.0 Dataset." *Journal of Peace Research* 50, no. 3 (May 1, 2013): 415–423.

CIDCM. "Minorities at Risk (MAR) Codebook Version," 2009. http://www.cidcm.umd.edu/mar/ (August 2018).

Collier, Paul, Anke Hoeffler, and Dominic Rohner. "Beyond Greed and Grievance. Feasibility and Civil War." *Oxford Economic Papers* 61, no. 1 (2009): 1–27.

DeRouen, Karl, Jacob Bercovitch, and Paulina Pospieszna. "Introducing the Civil Wars Mediation (CWM) Dataset." *Journal of Peace Research* 48, no. 5 (2011): 663–672.

Fearon, James D., and David D. Laitin. "Ethnicity, Insurgency and Civil War." *American Political Science Review* 97, no. 1 (2003): 75–96.

Festinger, Leon. "A Theory of Social Comparison Processes." *Human Relations* 7 (1954): 117–140.

Frank, Robert H. *Choosing the Right Pond: Human Behavior and the Quest for Status.* New York and Oxford: Oxford University Press, 1986.

Fukuyama, Francis. *Identity: The Demand for Dignity and the Politics of Resentment.* New York: Farrar, Straus and Giroux, 2018.

Ghai, Yash. *Autonomy and Ethnicity. Negotiating Competing Claims in Multi-Ethnic States.* Cambridge: Cambridge University Press, 2000.

Gurr, Ted Robert. *Why Men Rebel.* Princeton: Princeton University Press, 1970.

Henderson, Ailsa, and Nicola McEwen. "A Comparative Analysis of Voter Turnout in Regional Elections." *Electoral Studies* 29, no. 3 (2010): 405–416.

HIIK. "Heidelberg Institute for International Conflict Research," 2016. http://www.hiik.de/de/daten/ (June 2018).

Horowitz, Donald L. *Ethnic Groups in Conflict.* Los Angeles: University of California Press, 1985.

IWGIA. "International Work Group for Indigenous Affairs," 2016. http://www.iwgia.org/publications (June 2018).

Lapidoth, Ruth. *Autonomy: Flexible Solutions to Ethnic Conflicts.* Washington, DC: United States Institute of Peace Press, 1997.

Lehmbruch, Gerhard. *Proporzdemokratie. Politisches System und Politische Kultur in der Schweiz und in Österreich.* Tübingen: J.C.B Mohr, 1967.

Lemaine, Gérard. "Différenciation Sociale et Originalité Sociale." In *Expériences Entre Groupes*, edited by Willem Doise, 185–220, Paris: Mouton, 1970.

Lijphart, Arend. "Consociational Democracy." *World Politics* 21, no. 2 (1969): 207–225.

Minorities at Risk Project. "Minorities at Risk," 2009. http://www.mar.umd.edu/ (March 2017).

Minority Rights Group International. "World Directory of Minorities and Indigenous Peoples," 2016. http://minorityrights.org/directory/ (June 2018).

Nordquist, Kjell-Åke. "Autonomy as a Conflict-Solving Mechanism—An Overview." In *Autonomy. Applications and Implications*, edited by Markku Suksi. Dordrecht: Kluwer Law International, 1998.

Østby, Gudrun. "Polarization, Horizontal Inequalities and Violent Civil Conflict." *Journal of Peace Research* 45, no. 2 (2008): 143–162.

Reynal-Querol, Marta. "Ethnicity, Political Systems, and Civil Wars." *Journal of Conflict Resolution* 46, no. 1 (2002): 29–54.

Rørbæk, Lasse Lykke. "Killing in the Name of …? Types of Ethnic Groups and Armed Conflict." *Cooperation and Conflict* 52, no. 4 (2017): 537–552.

Saferworld. "Saferworld," 2016. http://www.saferworld.org.uk/ (August 2018).

Sambanis, Nicholas. "Do Ethnic and Nonethnic Civil Wars Have the Same Causes? A Theoretical and Empirical Inquiry." *The Journal of Conflict Resolution* 45, no. 3 (2001): 259–282.

Sanderson, Catherine A. *Social Psychology.* New York: John Wiley & Sons, 2009.

Schmidt, Manfred G. *Demokratietheorien. Eine Einführung.* Bonn: VS Verlag, 2010.

Schrijver, Frans Joachim. *Regionalism After Regionalisation: Spain, France and the United Kingdom*. Amsterdam: Vossiuspers, 2006.

Sherif, Muzafer, and Carolyn W. Sherif. *Social Psychology*. New York: Harper & Row, 1969.

Siroky, David S., and John Cuffe. "Lost Autonomy, Nationalism and Separatism." *Comparative Political Studies* 48, no. 1 (2015): 3–34.

Stewart, Frances. *Horizontal Inequalities: A Neglected Dimension of Development. Vol. 5. WIDER Annual Lectures*. Helsinki: United Nations University, World Institute for Development Economics Research, 2001.

———. *Horizontal Inequalities and Conflict. Understanding Group Violence in Multiethnic Societies*. London: Palgrave Macmillan, 2008.

Tajfel, Henri. *Human Groups and Social Categories*. London: Cambridge University Press, 1981.

———. "Social Categorization." In *Introduction á la Psychologie Sociale*, edited by Serge Moscovici, 272–302. Paris: Larousse, 1972.

Tajfel, Henri, and John C. Turner. "An Integrative Theory of Intergroup Conflict." In *The Social Psychology of Intergroup Relations*, edited by William G. Austin and Stephen Worchel, 33–47. Monterey, CA: Hall, 1979.

———. "The Social Identity Theory of Intergroup Behaviour." In *Psychology of Intergroup Relations*, edited by William G. Austin and Stephen Worchel, 7–24. Chicago: Hall, 1986.

Tocqueville, Alexis de. "Über die Demokratie in Amerika." In *Geschichte der Soziologie*, edited by Friedrich Jonas, 462–480. Opladen: VS Verlag, 1850.

Weber, Max. *Wirtschaft und Gesellschaft. Grundriss der Verstehenden Soziologie*. Tübingen: Mohr, 1921.

William, James. *The Principles of Psychology*. London and New York: Henry Holt & Company, 1890.

CHAPTER 3

A Set-Theoretical Analysis of Autonomy Success and Failure

The aim of this chapter is to understand which combinations of explanatory conditions account for the qualitative differences in post-conflict autonomy consolidation. In order to detect patterns of favorable and unfavorable conditions, the methodological tool of choice for the first empirical step is fuzzy-set Qualitative Comparative Analysis (fsQCA). QCA is based on a set-theoretical understanding of social phenomena and allows to deal with configurational forms of explanation. This makes it possible to include equifinal and conjunctural concepts of causality, and to take into account the high diversity of the autonomous regions in the sample. Sets are concepts of study, in which the cases of interest have a certain degree of (non-) membership. Set relations are usually interpreted in terms of necessary or sufficient conditions. A condition X is necessary, if, whenever the outcome Y is present, the condition is also present ($X \leftarrow Y$). The condition X must therefore be present for Y to occur. However, this does not imply that when X occurs, Y is given as well. This rather denotes a sufficient condition. A condition is sufficient if, whenever the condition is present, the outcome is also present ($X \rightarrow Y$). There is no case in which the condition is present and the outcome not.

Empirically, single conditions are rarely necessary or sufficient for a particular outcome but may unfold an effect only in combination with other conditions. It may also occur that a specific condition appears in different configurations, once in its presence and once in its absence. The same

F. Schulte, *Peace through Self-Determination*, Federalism and Internal Conflicts,
https://doi.org/10.1007/978-3-030-37587-4_3

factor can produce a different outcome, depending on the specific context in which it occurs, and the occurrence of an outcome can have a different explanation than its non-occurrence. Besides the consideration of such asymmetric relationships and a configurative understanding of social phenomena, which perfectly corresponds to the theoretical assumptions outlined above, QCA allows for equifinal explanations and the identification of different paths to autonomy success and failure. The determination of the membership values, the so-called calibration, is a critical step that involves a highly qualitative moment. It is therefore carried out in detail for each identified success condition in the following section.[1]

Operationalization and Calibration

Conflict Strategy (STRAGY)

The condition STRAGY is a multi-dimensional concept. It is based, on the one hand, on the general intensity of the ethnic conflict, like the weapons used by the rebels and state forces, personnel and, most importantly, casualties. On the other hand, the type of strategy depends on the primary political objective of the self-determination movement. The distinction between autonomy and secession claims by self-determination movements is, as mentioned, assessed on basis of statements by group elites or rebel organizations fighting on behalf of the group. The following case reports provide an illustrative overview of the conflict strategies applied in the self-determination conflicts in the cases of the sample.

Aceh

From the mid-1970s, the "Free Aceh Movement" (Gerakan Aceh Merdeka, GAM) fought violently for an independent state. In the nineteenth century, the Acehnese people resisted the incorporation of their sultanate into the Dutch colonial empire. Hoping for cultural self-determination, the group elites supported the Indonesian national movement. However, the newly created, yet unitarily organized and secular-oriented central state abruptly destroyed these hopes for cultural self-determination by merging the Muslim Aceh with the Christian North Sumatra region. The Darul Islam rebellion which was born out of this disappointment was temporarily defused in 1959 by granting some cultural

[1] The calibrated fuzzy scores are summarized in the Appendix.

rights to the Acehnese. In the 1970s, the industrializing central state began exploiting oil and gas deposits in the area, from which the local Acehnese hardly benefited. At the same time, minority rights turned out to be an empty promise under Suharto's rule. Consequently, the conflict escalated into ethnic civil war. The original demand for cultural autonomy gave way to the desire for full independence, which the founder of the GAM movement, Hasan di Tiro, proclaimed for the first time in 1976. The government sought to contain the secessionist movement with a massive military presence in the region and declared Aceh a military operation zone, which was a carte blanche for arbitrary arrests, forced evictions, and systematic rape, to which GAM also responded with attacks on police and military posts. Due to the high conflict intensity and ethnic demands for independence, the case is calibrated with the fuzzy score of 0.

Åland

After more than 650 years under Swedish rule, the Åland Islands fell to the Russian Grand Duchy of Finland in 1809. Already during the February Revolution, a movement calling for the reunification with the Swedish motherland emerged on Åland. In the Finnish Civil War, the Swedish kin-state sent troops with the justification that the goal was to protect the language and culture of the local population. The Finnish side opposed the call for a plebiscite but was willing to declare Swedish the only language allowed on the islands. However, the Åland movement insisted on reunification, whereupon the leaders of the movement were charged with treason. The outbreak of violence, or even an interstate war, could have been prevented by the agreement to let the League of Nations decide on the Åland situation. After British mediation efforts, the League of Nations declared that Åland would remain an integral part of the Finnish state. However, the population was to receive territorial self-government, the islands were to remain demilitarized, and the territory would also receive neutral status. While Sweden and Finland accepted this ruling in 1921, most Ålanders rejected the autonomy status. However, the acceptance of territorial self-governance was growing constantly and the Åland Parliament approved a revision of the statute both in 1951 and in 1993 by a large majority. Since the self-determination movement acted peacefully, the secession claim was dropped over time, and both sides finally accepted the compromise solution, the case is calibrated with the fuzzy score of 0.9.

Atlantic Regions

Its Anglo-Protestant character, combined with geographical seclusion, led to the political and cultural isolation of Nicaragua's Atlantic coast. The Sandinista National Liberation Front (FSLN), which replaced the Samoza regime in 1979, attempted to impose the Spanish-dominated national culture on the ethnically heterogeneous region. Literacy campaigns were initially met with approval from the ethnic organization MISURASATA (Miskito, Sumo, Rama, Sandinista Asla Takanka [united]). As the organization gained importance, it began to raise self-determination demands. These alarmed the central government when CIA-backed Sandinist groups gathered at the Honduran border. When some MISURASATA leaders were arrested in February 1981, ethnic tensions escalated. The central government responded to the group's guerilla attacks by mass expulsions, arbitrary arrests, torture, and killings. Ethnic splinter groups sided with the Contra rebels and plunged the country into civil war. The violent clashes between the ethnic groups of the Atlantic coast and the central government significantly lost in intensity, as the MISURASATA itself proposed the creation of an autonomous region in 1985. After tough negotiations, the central government accepted the offer, and the Región Autonoma Atlantico Norte (RAAN) and the Región Autonoma Atlantico Sur (RAAS) were created. The groups demanded autonomy but tried to enforce it violently. However, since the self-determination conflict was less violent than the parallel Contra conflict and both sides showed cooperative behavior in the peace process, the case is calibrated with the fuzzy score of 0.7.

Basque Country

The Basques already enjoyed extensive privileges in the Spanish-Castilian kingdom in the twelfth century. However, this cultural autonomy was largely curtailed in the course of the administrative centralization of Spain in the nineteenth century. This resulted in the emergence of a nationalist movement, which soon led to the founding of the Basque Nationalist Party (Partido Nacionalista Vasco, PNV). Initial demands for an independent Basque country were already made at the beginning of the twentieth century. The simmering tensions erupted in the Spanish Civil War in which the Basques fought on the Republican side against the centralist-oriented and anti-pluralist putschists led by General Franco. Franco's victory in 1939 led to the suppression of all political and cultural activities of the Basque minority, which did not fit into the picture of an ethnically homogeneous unitary state. Repressions and massive assimilation pressure led to the radicalization of the self-determination movement and the founding of the underground organization Euskadi Ta Askatasuna (ETA). After an initially peaceful resistance, ETA began to act violently starting in 1986 with shootings, bombings, and attacks on police and military. With the transition of Spain, the region received a special territorial status in the democratic constitution. However, ETA and its political wing rejected the autonomy offer and tried to enforce a separate state with a strategy of systematic and offensive violence against state forces. In turn, the central government responded with a repressive strategy and paramilitary actions against the separatists. Basque support for ETA terror is steadily decreasing, especially following the implementation of the autonomy system. However, the radical wing did not decide for the primacy of conventional politics until 2010 and only recently was the organization completely disarmed.

Bodoland

The cultural autonomy demanded already during colonial times was again on the political agenda of the All Bodo Students Union (ABSU) in the 1970s. In parallel with the Bodos' aspirations for autonomy, a militant movement of the dominant Assamese fought against the mass immigration of predominantly Muslim Bengalis into the sub-state. Assamese nationalism was increasingly perceived as a threat and led to a radicalization of the Bodo movement. The initial demands for autonomy became demands for their own sub-state or, in the radical wing, for full independence. In 1989, militant Bodos, organized in the Bodoland Security Force (BdSF), began attacking villages and state institutions, and killing Assamese and immigrant groups. After lengthy negotiations, the regional government decided in 1993 to set up a local self-governing council. However, armed insurgent groups, such as the National Democratic Front of Bodoland (NDFB) or the Bodo Liberation Tigers (BLT), began attacking all non-Bodos in the region, which consequently led to an intensification of the conflict. Peace negotiations between the central government, the regional government, and the BLT finally ended with the creation of the Bodoland Territorial Area Districts (BTAD) as a conflict-regulating territorial autonomy arrangement in February 2003. However, demands for an independent Bodoland have not disappeared.

Bougainville

The German and Australian colonial rulers ignored the lack of a supra-regional community feeling as well as the postcolonial nation-state did. Bougainville was allocated to Papua New Guinea irrespective of its geographical and historical-cultural proximity to the Solomon Islands. As early as 1968, a movement on the islands grew that called for the separation from the central state in order to return to traditional leadership rather than being governed under the unfamiliar Westminster model. In fact, the independent Republic of the Northern Salomon Islands was proclaimed in 1975. First, the government in Port Moresby was able to convince the Bougainvilleans to remain a province in the central state. But when a state copper mine caused severe environmental degradation in the settlement area and a mass influx of non-indigenous workers, ethnic tensions escalated. First acts of sabotage by the Bougainville Revolutionary Army (BRA) led to a military intervention. The BRA renewed its secessionist claims and underlined them with a highly violent strategy. The central government imposed a blockade on the territory and committed numerous human rights violations on the indigenous population. Since the state forces failed to stop the insurgents' guerilla attacks, the central government hired foreign mercenaries. When this was exposed by the Australian media outlets, the country sank into chaos and violence in 1997. After about a year, a ceasefire was negotiated. Increasing divisions within the BRA and mediation efforts by neighboring Australia, New Zealand, Fiji, and Vanuatu paved the way for the first, constitutionally recognized, autonomous government called the Bougainville Reconciliation Government before a People's Congress took over governmental affairs in 1999. In 2001, after protracted negotiations, the parties agreed on a peace agreement and a regional autonomy solution to settle the Bougainville conflict.

Catalonia

By the end of the ninth century, the Counts of Barcelona were independent, but as the Catalans sided with Charles of Habsburg in the War of Spanish Succession, they lost their historic powers after the victory of Phillip of Bourbon and had to submit to the centralized system of the absolutist ruler. It was not until the nineteenth century that a cultural reawakening took place. Although nourished by the recovery of the Catalan economy as a supplier to warring parties in the First World War, the explicitly expressed goal of regaining historical independence remained an unfulfilled wish. The hopes of gaining self-determination in the Restoration era were also bitterly disappointed when instead, Catalan symbols were banned, and the public use of the language was forbidden under the rule of Primo de Rivera. As in other cases, social and cultural marginalization had led to a strengthening of the self-determination movement. A few hours before the declaration of the Second Spanish Republic in 1931, the Catalan leader Francesc Macià proclaimed a Catalan Republic. The Catalans, however, were willing to compromise and accepted cultural autonomy rights. However, the established administrative autonomy was suspended again in 1934 and finally dissolved after the victory of Franco in 1939. In the authoritarian period, the Catalans were exposed to severe repression and faced executions, arbitrary arrests, language bans, and forced assimilation through replacements of Catalan names and inscriptions. While there was no violent counter-strategy, the demands for independence have never disappeared and have received new impetus in recent years.

Chittagong Hill Tracts

Under British colonial rule, the Chittagong Hill Tracts (CHT) enjoyed a special administrative status which was lost under Pakistani rule. Far-reaching exploitation of natural resources and the expulsion of hundreds of thousands from their ancestral land caused strong grievances among the indigenous peoples. In independent Bangladesh, Jumma elites demanded self-government rights and the constitutional recognition of their ethnic identity. These claims were rejected by the central government, which demanded that ethnic groups adapt to the Bengali majority culture. The Jumma organization Parbatya Chattagram Jana Samhati Samiti (PCJSS) first tried to achieve the goal of cultural self-determination peacefully. As uprisings were struck down bloodily, the PCJSS military arm, the Shanti Bahini, began attacking state institutions, military posts, and non-indigenous villages. The conflict was widening into a full-blown civil war when the government began to militarize the whole area, accompanied by hundreds of thousands of Bengalis, which were part of a resettlement program to accelerate the re-nationalization of the Jumma. Both sides used a highly violent strategy. There were guerilla attacks of the Shanti Bahini on Bengali settlers and massacres, in addition to torture and the expulsion of indigenous people by the state army and paramilitary settler groups. After more than 25 years, a peace treaty was signed that underlines the uncompromising attitude of all involved parties.

Corsica
Once under the control of Genoa, the Corsicans won their independence in 1730. After a short monarchist intermezzo, the Corsicans created one of the first written democratic constitutions. Soon after, though, the region fell to France. Mistrust toward the central state and minor riots against central authorities remained virulent over the centuries. Only in the 1960s, however, was a broad resistance movement against centralism and for an economic modernization of the backward island formed. It was not until about a decade later that regionalist parties, such as the Front régionaliste corse (FRC) and the Action pour renaissance de la Corse (ARC) articulated cultural-political demands. The arrival of thousands of Frenchmen from Algeria after the lost Algerian war finally resulted in a strong antagonism against the majority population. With government support, migrants settled and farmed sparse land and the Corsicans feared becoming a minority on their own island. Organizations like the ARC and in particular the Fronte di Liberazione Naziunale Corsu (FLNC), founded in 1976, radicalized and turned toward a strategy of violence in the struggle of the "Corsican question". In the early 1970s, the number of bomb attacks on governmental buildings and mainland French tourist facilities rose rapidly. The situation climaxed in 1998 with the murder of the French prefect, to which the central government reacted by sending paramilitary forces. Stages of relative calm alternated with times of frequent bomb explosions. However, Corsican nationalism did not produce a homogeneous self-determination movement with unified demands. Although today an overwhelming majority opposes an independent Corsica, secessionist demands continue to be voiced by various splinter groups.

Gagauzia
In the course of the Russian-Ottoman wars of the eighteenth century, the Gagauz migrated to present-day Moldova, where the minority group was exposed to repressions and heavy assimilation pressure under Tsarist, Soviet, and especially Romanian rule. In the wake of the collapse of the USSR, the Popular Front of Moldova emerged, in which Moldovan and Gagauz elites jointly strove for an emancipation from Moscow. Moldovan elites soon preferred to join Romania, however. The non-Moldovan groups saw their cultural identity in danger and feared renewed Romanian repression. Protests against the nationalist tendencies and demands for self-government increased in their settlement areas Gagauzia and Transnistria. After the central state declared its sovereignty, Transnistria

also declared its independence and initiated a hitherto unresolved violent secessionist conflict. The Gagauz national movement also proclaimed its own Soviet Republic in November 1989. After a rally of about 40,000 Moldovans to prevent the first Gagauz elections, the formation of Gagauz paramilitaries, and first clashes, another secessionist conflict was imminent in the country. Both sides have not pursued a violent strategy but had engaged in peaceful negotiations on institutional reforms. Not least because of the developments in Transnistria and the emergence of a de facto independent state there, the economic weakness and the low strategic importance of the Gagauz settlement areas, in which neither Russian military nor weapons and arsenals were stored, moderate and escalation-averse forces retained the upper hand. When the country's first president, Mircea Snegur, clearly opposed reunification and independence, and the Gagauz elites gradually moved away from their initial secessionist aspirations, the foundation was already set for the region's autonomous status, adopted in 1994.

Gilgit-Baltistan

Until 1848, the valleys in northern Pakistan were small kingdoms in the midst of the world's highest mountain ranges. After 1848, these kingdoms were incorporated into the princely state of Kashmir under the rule of the Dogra. After the retreat of the British colonial rulers, the Kashmiri Maharaja decided to join India. A violent rebellion by the Gilgit Scouts in November 1947 led to the withdrawal of Kashmiri troops from the territory inhabited by Gilgiti, Balti, and Hunza. The movement led by Raja Shah Rais Khan proclaimed an independent Republic of Gilgit. However, when an attack by Indian troops became apparent, the ethnic leaders decided to seek support from Pakistan. Despite initially strong pro-Pakistani preferences among the local population, this decision was taken at the elite level and lacked broad mass-level support. Pakistan annexed the area without integrating it into its state structure and ruled from then on with police laws. It was not until 1970 when the "Northern Areas" institutions were created, which were transformed into a regional autonomy system nearly 40 years later. From the 1950s onward, there were repeated violent protests from numerous parties and movements, such as the Balawaristan National Front (BNF), the Gilgit Baltistan United Movement (GBUM), or the Gilgit Baltistan National Alliance (GBNA). Their demands range from autonomy rights to full independence of the historic Balawaristan region.

Guna Yala

The Kuna on Panama's northern coast survived the period of Spanish colonialism with a relatively weak assimilation to the majority culture. Already in 1871, a decree created the Comarca de Tulanega that granted the Kuna de facto independence. When their mother land became independent in 1903, the minority group placed great hopes in the central government for it to take account of their political autonomy and traditional way of life. When these hopes were disappointed and more and more Christian missionaries and workers entered the region after the completion of the Panama Canal, the Kuna revolted to defend their ethnic identity and traditional institutions. The rebellion in 1925 was directed against state officials, in particular the Panamanian police, who tried to eradicate the "barbaric customs" of the indigenous people. However, since the level of violence was rather low compared to other cases of the sample, the conflict is coded as a crisis. On February 8, 1925, the Kuna, under the leadership of Nele Kantule, declared the independence of their ancestral territory as the Republic of Tule. Two years later, talks between Kuna leaders and government officials began, mediated by the United States. Both sides were willing to compromise, and the Kuna accepted the sovereignty and the territorial integrity of Panama. The central government delegated first self-determination rights in 1930. With the implementation of the Comarca Kuna Yala in 1953, the ethnic group received territorial self-governance in the sense of the stated criteria.

Jammu and Kashmir

The former princely state enjoyed extensive sovereignty under British rule. From 1925, the Maharajah Hari Singh of the Hindu Dogra dynasty ruled over the mainly Muslim population. In the 1930s, a protest movement formed which emphasized the distinctiveness of the Muslim-Kashmiri identity and resisted the repressive rule of the ruler. After minor violent uprisings, a rebellion broke out against the royal family in 1947. In the wake of Pakistan's and India's independence in the same year, the Maharajah was faced with the decision of joining one of the states or remaining independent. In the face of the ongoing Kashmiri insurrection against monarchic rule and the infiltration of Pakistani fighters, the ruler sought help from India and immediately declared Kashmir's accession to the Indian Union. The battles between the Indian army and the insurgents soon also involved the Pakistani army. From the moment of independence, the conflict, which escalated several times into an interstate war, had both a domestic and an interstate dimension. The constitution of the independent India granted the region far-reaching autonomy rights, which, however, were never fully implemented. When Prime Minister Abdullah brought the territory's independence back on the agenda in 1953, the special status was almost completely eroded. Repressions by the central state increased group grievances. When massive electoral fraud became public knowledge during the 1987 election, which was directed primarily against the Muslim United Front (MUF), violence escalated. The frustration fueled by the mix of denied self-determination, religious polarization, corruption, and low opportunity costs led to a violent uprising. The rebellion was initially supported by the Jammu and Kashmir Liberation Front (JKLF). As the independence demands of the JKLF soon displeased the Pakistani supporters, Islamic groups like Hizb-ul-Mujahideen (HM) and Jaish-e-Mohammed (JeM) shifted their focus. A third line of conflict between different religious groups developed in the area. Unlike the ethnic Kashmiri organizations, these groups advocate for the annexation of Kashmir to Pakistan and a stronger Islamization of the region.

Kurdistan

In the Ottoman Empire, the Kurdish rulers had a relatively high degree of sovereignty. The empire's defeat in the First World War, however, led to a fragmentation of the settlement area. The option of a Kurdish state formulated in the 1920 Treaty of Sèvres fell victim to emerging Turkish nationalism and was never seriously considered. Consequently, five million Kurds found themselves in the UK-mandated Kingdom of Iraq. With the beginning of the incorporation, opposition grew against the British-Iraqi rule, leading to several uprisings and, finally, to the proclamation of the Kingdom of Kurdistan in 1922. However, the attempt to establish an independent Kurdish nation-state quickly failed due to the uncompromising reaction of the colonial power. Although the tribal society had only developed a weak Kurdish identity at that time, a broad secessionist movement emerged. The strategy was based on an armed struggle from the beginning. As a result of the Second World War, the Kurds seemed to benefit from Soviet influence in neighboring Iran. Not far from the border, the Kurdish Republic of Mahabad was founded in 1946. After the withdrawal of the USSR, this state founding project also failed after only a few months. The establishment of the Iraqi republic in 1958 improved relations between the two groups which were considered equal under the new constitution. However, strong nationalist aspirations on both sides fueled tensions that escalated into a civil war. Peace talks ended in 1970 with the establishment of the Autonomous Kurdistan Region. But the poor implementation of the reforms, unclear demarcations, the possession of oil fields, and the instrumentalization of the actors in the course of the Cold War led to a renewed escalation. The second Iraqi-Kurdish war ended in 1975 with several thousand casualties and a capitulation of the Peshmerga. In the course of the Iran-Iraq war in the 1980s, the Baath Party responded to the alliance of some Kurdish groups with Iran with genocidal repressions. In the wake of the Second Gulf War in 1991, there was another rebellion against the dictatorship of Saddam Hussein. Due to the countermeasures of the Iraqi army, a protection zone was set up under the supervision of the Western Allies, under whose protection the Kurdish territorial autonomy was established.

Mindanao

Mindanao was under the rule of Muslim sultanates until the sixteenth century, before the country fell under Spanish rule in 1565. While the inhabitants of the main islands were quickly and sustainably colonized and Christianized, the efforts of the colonial rulers further south were largely failing, due to the persistent resistance of the local Moro. For more than 300 years, the Muslim Moro resisted rather peacefully against Spanish power claims on the southern archipelago. The resistance was finally broken with increased repressive measures by the Spaniards and, in particular, the Americans, as a colonial successor after the Spanish-American War in 1889. For the exploitation and control of the resource-rich territory, land use rights were granted to Christianized settlers from the north. After the Second World War, violent clashes were rare and limited to local feuds. This changed in the 1960s when the central government made Christians from the north settle in the "wild south," resulting in dramatic demographic changes. Through this Philippinization, the Moro saw their culture threatened and feared becoming a minority in their ancestral lands. The clashes between settlers and indigenous Moro became more frequent as the police and military of the central state, which had become independent in 1946, began to strengthen the positions of migrants. After the Jabidah massacre of 1968, in which several Moro recruits were executed by the state army, the ethnic conflict escalated. The Muslim Independence Movement (MIM) and the Moro National Liberation Front (MNLF) demanded a separate Moro nation (Bangsamoro), whereas the latter took up an armed struggle against the central state. The civil war between Muslims, the Christian "Ilaga" organization, and the state army killed about 50,000 people. Both a military stalemate and international pressure led to the Treaty of Tripoli in 1976, which provided an autonomy solution for the historic Moroland. Due to various differences over the interpretation of the peace agreement, the MNLF rejected the offer and renewed their demands for independence. This resulted in massive internal unrest within the Moro movement, from which the Moro Islamic Liberation Front (MILF) emerged as the main rebel organization. After the fall of Marcos, the central government offered the Moro territorial self-governance and implemented the Autonomous Region in Muslim Mindanao (ARMM) in 1989. Despite the transfer of self-determination rights, further peace negotiations, and several revisions, the conflict could not yet be ended. Moro factions, such as the Bangsamoro Islamic Freedom Movement (BIFM) or the Bangsamoro Islamic Freedom Fighters (BIFF) still adhere to an armed strategy for achieving their own Islamic state.

New Caledonia

The colonization of the archipelago began with the settlement of Christian missionaries in 1840. Shortly after, the French colonialists established a penal colony in New Caledonia. Tens of thousands of prisoners were brought to the remote island. The guarding and bureaucracy of the penal colony required the migration of non-native workers. The number of non-indigenous people soon exceeded the number of ethnic Kanaks. The indigenous clan society shrank as a result of imported diseases. The Kanak experienced a strong marginalization through an Apartheid-like system based on the so-called Code de l'indigénat, which restricted freedom of movement, contained forced labor, created a poll tax, and limited the right to ownership of land. The grievances led to smaller riots, which were mainly directed against the expropriation of traditional settlement land and the extensive cattle farming of the settlers, which threatened traditional agricultural practices. A major rebellion, the "Great Revolt," in which about 1200 Indigenous people and several hundred settlers were killed, took place in 1878. The colonial rulers reacted with repressive measures. As a result, the Kanak continued their violent strategy in several minor uprisings that were all quelled by security forces. After the Second World War, New Caledonia was declared an overseas territory. The short-term granting of some administrative rights was reversed after just a few months. The economic boom in the 1960s, which mainly benefitted the white population, and the mass migration of Europeans led to renewed polarization. After various indigenous student protests, an independence movement organized in the Kanak and Socialist National Liberation Front (FLNKS) demanded its own state system, which was proclaimed in December 1984. The self-determination movement used a violent strategy that included attacks on settlers and state institutions, looting, and pillaging. The central government reacted repressively with the imposition of the state of emergency, including curfews and the sending in of the military. The conflict culminated in the violent taking hostage of several police officers by separatists and their liberation by the military. After this event, however, the parties were ready to negotiate institutional reforms. Already in 1988, the Treaty of Matignon initiated the territorial self-government and modernization of the island. The secession demands remain virulent and culminated in an independence referendum in November 2018.

Northern Ireland

Catholic-Gaelic Ireland was subordinated to the reformed Protestant-English kingdom in 1541. The settlement of Protestant settlers, especially in the northeast of the island, provoked early Irish resistance. The economic and political marginalization cast into legal forms with the "penal laws" intensified the disparity between the religious groups. Only after over 300 years of resistance, which culminated in the War of Independence (1919–1921), did the "home rule" movement reach its goal: the establishment of the Irish Free State. The price of Irish sovereignty, negotiated under the Anglo-Irish Treaty of 1921, was that the predominantly Protestant and economically prosperous Northern Territories remain part of the United Kingdom. In Northern Ireland, Catholics found themselves in a Protestant-dominated entity with limited self-administrative competencies. The latter still feel that they belong to Britain as "Unionists," opposed by Catholic Republicans and their desire to reunify the whole of Ireland. The opposing demands mingled with various political, economic, and social discrimination—ranging from multiple voting rights for Unionist landowners in local elections, gerrymandering in favor of the majority population, to the allocation of jobs and housing and positions in the loyalist-dominated security forces. After years of fragile peace, a civil rights movement emerged in the 1960s. The initially peaceful social protests soon tore open old wounds. After the first street battles, radical voices gained weight on both sides. The loyalists interpreted the protests as attacks on "their" state and formed organizations, such as the Ulster

Constitution Defense Committee (UCDC) and the paramilitary Ulster Protestant Volunteers (UPV). As further demonstrations were violently halted by the Protestant-dominated security forces, "the troubles" escalated into a civil war. Especially after the "Bloody Sunday" of 1972, the initially poorly organized Republicans backed the Irish Republican Army (IRA), which used a violent strategy to fight the unionist paramilitaries and national security forces. The central government responded with imprisonment, the withdrawal of self-government rights, and the deployment of the military. In bombing, shootings, and arson attacks, over 3000 people were killed between 1968 and 1998. Despite the Good Friday Agreement of 1998 and a marked decline in violence, the conflict is still virulent.

South Tyrol

South Tyrol was part of the Habsburg monarchy for centuries, before both Italian-speaking Trentino and today's South Tyrol, with its largely German-speaking population, fell to Italy as war booty after the First World War. The hopes for the protection of South Tyrolean identity had to be buried with Mussolini's seizure of power. In the course of the Italianization, German schools and parties were banned, and even grave inscriptions and surnames were replaced by Italian names. A massive influx of Italians was to ensure the dominance of the titular nation in the region. The final act was the resettlement measures negotiated between Mussolini and Hitler. South Tyroleans were given the "option" of either emigrating to the neighboring German Reich or remaining in Fascist Italy and being forcibly integrated into the mainstream Italian culture, losing their language and cultural heritage. After the war, the South Tyrolean People's Party (SVP) brought ethnic self-determination back on the agenda. Although the Allies refused independence, they insisted on protection for the non-Italian language groups. An agreement was reached during the Paris peace negotiations. However, instead of transferring the competencies to the province of Bolzano as the main settlement area of the ethnic group, the larger Trentino province was empowered, which secured the titular nation its political and demographic overweight in the region. After initial peaceful demonstrations for self-determination and the end of continued immigration, the first bombs of the Befreiungsausschuss Südtirol (BAS) exploded in 1956. The focus of the activities was on the destruction of state infrastructure and fascist monuments. Despite a number of casualties, arbitrary arrests, and torture, the conflict remained at a low level of intensity. In 1959, Austria brought the case to the United Nations, which called on the parties to solve the conflict. A parliamentary commission elaborated a second statute of autonomy, which was accepted by the SVP and the Austrian government and ratified by the Italian Parliament.

Zanzibar

After a short Portuguese intermezzo, Zanzibar became a prosperous economic center under the rule of the Sultan of Oman. After the division of the Omani dominion, the region could no longer resist European attempts to exert political influence. During the colonial period, a hierarchical social structure developed, headed by Omani Arab landowners and Indian traders, whereas the majority of the population consisted of impoverished peasants and workers of mainly African origin. The strong asymmetries in society led to several workers' riots in the 1950s. Anti-colonial sentiments in the wake of the emerging pan-African nationalism provided a manifestation of the social cleavages that led to the establishment of the first ethnic organizations in the 1920s. The Arab-dominated Zanzibar Nationalist Party (ZNP) advocated the independence of the island under the rule of the sultan. Their counterparts included the anti-Arab, Tanganyika-backed Afro Shirazi Party (ASP) and the Zanzibar and Pemba People's Party (ZPPP), which represented the interests of the Persian Shirazi on the archipelago island Pemba. In December 1961, the colonial power granted Tanganyika independence and the region became a constitutional monarchy under the rule of the Sultan. Although the SPA won the elections held in 1957, the party was kept out of government by electoral fraud. Dissatisfaction with the dominance of the Arab elite finally erupted in a violent coup in 1964. Led by the ASP Youth League, the sultan was overthrown and tens of thousands of Zanzibaris' of Arab and Indian descent were forcibly displaced. The revolutionary government proclaimed the Socialist People's Republic of Zanzibar and Pemba in January 1964. The coup escalated into a civil war with an estimated death toll between 2,000 and 15,000. For reasons of strategical interest and fears of a counter-coup, Tanganyika's president convinced the ethnic leaders to found a united Tanzania, in which Zanzibar received autonomy status. Secession is still demanded by Arab-Muslim organizations such as the Civic United Front (CUF) or the Islamic Movement Uamsho, which often provokes violent counter-demonstrations.

The fuzzy scores assigned for the condition of the conflict strategy (STRAGY) via the qualitative assessment of the conflict histories are

Table 3.1 Fuzzy scores for STRAGY

Case	*Highest conflict intensity*	*Demands*	*Fuzzy score*
ACH	War	Secession	0
ALA	Dispute	Secession	0.9
ATL	Violent Crisis	Autonomy	0.7
BAS	Violent Crisis	Secession	0.4
BOD	Limited War	Secession	0.2
BOU	Limited War	Secession	0.2
CAT	Dispute	Secession	0.8
CHT	War	Autonomy	0.1
COR	Violent Crisis	Secession	0.4
GAG	Crisis	Secession	0.7
GIL	Violent Crisis	Secession	0.3
GUN	Crisis	Secession	0.7
JAM	War	Secession	0
KUR	War	Secession	0
MIN	Limited War	Secession	0.2
CAL	Violent Crisis	Secession	0.4
IRL	Limited War	Secession	0.2
TIR	Violent Crisis	Autonomy	0.6
SAN	Limited War	Secession	0.2

displayed in Table 3.1. The calibration results show that a large number of autonomy reforms were indeed preceded by secessionist conflicts, of which a large number experienced violence. Only in three cases were only autonomy demands raised (ATL, CHT, TIR). Only in four cases of the sample (ALA, CAT, GAG, GUN) did the actors rely solely on peaceful means.

Scope of Autonomy (SCOPE)

The degree of autonomy is a notoriously difficult concept to measure. Nevertheless, empirical research on regionalism and federalism has identified a plethora of indicators and has produced a rapidly growing number of data sets in recent years.[2] Measurement approaches such as the Localization and Decentralization Index (Ivanyna/Shah 2014), the Local Autonomy Index (Ladner et al. 2016), or the Regional Authority Index (Hooghe et al. 2016) typically analyze the de jure transferred political and

[2] Harguindéguy, Cole, and Pasquier, "The Variety of Decentralization Indexes".

fiscal competencies and draw conclusions about the strength and independence of subnational units.[3] These approaches have some shortcomings. They usually do not take into account whether the guaranteed level of competencies is actually achieved or whether the transferred powers merely exist on paper. However, this is not irrelevant, as discrepancies between the de jure and de facto degrees of autonomy can be extreme, as shown by numerous cases such as Tibet, Tatarstan, or Palestine. Almost all existing approaches show strong Eurocentrism and Western-bias, which leads to a considerable number of sub-state regions in the sample, especially those in defective democracies or autocracies, being not covered by existing data sets. In addition, neither the characteristics of ethnic territories nor the specifics of territorial autonomies are considered by existing operationalizations. There is usually no distinction made between different forms of vertical power sharing, although there are, as outlined in the introductory chapter, important differences between federalism, decentralization, and territorial autonomy in terms of design and performance.[4]

For these reasons, this study uses an alternative measurement method for the calibration of SCOPE. In order to take into account both the de jure and the de facto level of regional authority, a two-stage procedure is applied. First, the current autonomy law in force is analyzed applying qualitative content analysis to determine whether the regional government has legal competencies on the six key dimensions of ethnic empowerment introduced in Chap. 2. In a second step, each case is closely reviewed to ensure that the granted powers can actually be exercised by the regional authorities.

Decisive for the measurement of the de jure competence level is the question whether the regional government can pass binding rules through legislation or executive orders and thus enjoys exclusive-authoritative powers. For culture (CUL) as a highly important policy dimension from an identity-theoretical point of view, this concerns language and religion legislation as well as the protective rights of education in the native language and the right to use own symbols. For the security dimension (SEC), it is, as outlined above, essential whether local residents have free access to the judiciary or whether local or traditional courts exist. In

[3] Ivanyna and Shah, "How Close Is Your Government to Its People?"; Ladner, Keuffer, and Baldersheim, "Measuring Local Autonomy in 39 Countries (1990–2014)"; Hooghe et al., *Measuring Regional Authority*.

[4] Schulte and Trinn, "Untangling Autonomy."

addition, the existence of regional police or security forces is taken into account. The measurement of the financial dimension (FIN) follows the coding scheme of the Regional Authority Index and examines whether a regional government can levy local taxes and has budgetary and credit rights.[5] High fuzzy scores are assigned if the regional government can levy own "major taxes" such as personal income, value added, and sales tax. In the case of low fuzzy scores, the regional government does not enjoy financial autonomy or can levy only "minor taxes".

While adequate funding is essential for operating in various policy fields, the social dimension (SOC) is again directly relevant to ethnic recognition. High values are given when there is a functioning and self-financed education and health system in the autonomous region that is able to provide sufficient social goods to the local population. High values on the international dimension (INT) imply that the autonomous government can independently conclude international treaties, has the right to veto if international treaties affect exclusive areas of autonomy, and has the right to join international or regional organizations. The final dimension CON is the safeguard dimension that does not cover a specific policy area but rather the specific guarantee of the region. It takes into account the existence of bodies that can mediate in conflicts between state tiers. Furthermore, the calibration includes whether the special status of the region in enshrined in constitutional law. Table 3.2 gives a detailed overview of the coding and assignment of the exact fuzzy scores of the de jure measurement.

The next step is to examine whether the de jure values assigned actually apply. The case-based evaluation is based on the following three qualitative indicators:

1. The regional government has been involved in policy-making in one of the six policy fields (*yes/no*).
2. Policy issues that can be attributed to one of the six policy dimensions were debated in the regional assembly or addressed by regional political parties (*yes/no*).
3. The regional budget provides for expenditures on the specific dimension (*yes/no*).

[5] Hooghe, Marks, and Schakel, *The Rise of Regional Authority: A Comparative Study of 42 Democracies.*

Table 3.2 Coding scheme for SCOPE

Dimension	*Operationalization*	*Values*
Culture (CUL)	No competence in (a), (b), (c), and (d), whereby (a) language legislation, (b) religion legislation, (c) right to education in native language, and (d) right to use own symbols	0
	Weak competence in (a), (b), (c), or (d)	0.5
	Weak competence in (a), (b), (c), and (d)	1
	Authoritative competence in (a) or (b)	1.5
	Authoritative competence in (a) and (b)	2
	Authoritative competence in (a) and (b) and (c) or (d)	2.5
	Authoritative competence in (a), (b), (c), and (d)	3
Security (SEC)	No security competencies	0
	Regional traditional courts or limited access to national courts	0.5
	Regional traditional courts and free access to national courts	1
	Regional traditional courts and free access to national courts and consultation on security issues	1.5
	Regional public order service under the authority of state police forces and traditional courts or free access to national courts	2
	Regional police forces under authority of state police forces and traditional courts or free access to national courts	2.5
	Regional police forces and traditional courts or free access to national courts	3
Finance (FIN)	No fiscal competencies	0
	Regional government sets rate of at least one minor tax	0.5
	Regional government sets base and rate of minor taxes	1
	Regional government sets rate of at least one major tax	1.5
	Regional government sets rate of at least one major tax and has budgetary rights	2
	Regional government sets rate of at least one major tax, has budgetary rights and can borrow with authorization from the central state	2.5
	Regional government sets rate of at least one major tax, has budgetary rights and can borrow without restrictions from the central state	3
Social (SOC)	No social-political competencies	0
	Consultation of regional government on education and health issues	0.5
	Weak competencies in education or health policy	1
	Weak competencies in education and health policy	1.5
	Regional health or education system with state subsidies	2
	Regional health and education system with state subsidies	2.5
	Self-financed regional health or education system	3

(*continued*)

Table 3.2 (continued)

Dimension	*Operationalization*	*Values*
International (INT)	No international competencies	0
	Consultation of regional government on international issues	0.5
	Veto-rights and consultation of regional government on international issues	1
	Right to conclude international treaties with authorization from the central state	1.5
	Right to conclude international treaties without authorization from the central state	2
	Right to conclude international treaties with authorization from the central state or accession right to international organizations	2.5
	Right to conclude international treaties with authorization from the central state and accession right to international organizations	3
Safeguard/Constitution (CON)	No special safeguarding	0
	Ad hoc mediation instance	0.5
	Institutionalized mediation instance	1
	Constitutional entrenchment or autonomy statute with constitutional status	1.5
	Constitutional entrenchment and ad hoc mediation instance	2
	Constitutional entrenchment and institutionalized mediation instance	2.5
	Autonomy statute with constitutional status and institutionalized mediation instance	3

Due to the availability of reliable data, only a limited period between January and December 2016 is taken into account. Where there are no indications of any sub-state activity regarding one of the three indicators in the period, the corresponding dimension is coded as "0". The values of the six dimensions are standardized into the Autonomy Scope Index, which delivers the fuzzy values for the condition SCOPE (Table 3.3).[6]

[6] Schulte, "The More, The Better? Assessing the Scope of Regional Autonomy as a Key Condition for Ethnic Conflict Regulation."

Table 3.3 Fuzzy scores for SCOPE

Case	*CUL*	*SEC*	*FIN*	*SOC*	*INT*	*CON*	*TOTAL*	*SCOPE*
ACH	2.5	2	3	2.5	2	1.5	13.5	0.75
ALA	3	2.5	3	3	3	3	17.5	0.97
ATL	2.5	1.5	1	2	0	1.5	8.5	0.47
BAS	2.5	3	3	3	3	2	16.5	0.92
BOD	1	0.5	1.5	2	0	1.5	6.5	0.36
BOU	1.5	2	1	3	1.5	3	12	0.67
CAL	2.5	2.5	3	3	2	2	15	0.83
CAT	2.5	3	3	3	3	2	16.5	0.92
CHT	1	0.5	0.5	1	0	0	3	0.17
COR	1	0	1	0	1.5	1	4.5	0.25
GAG	2.5	2	0.5	3	2	2.5	12.5	0.69
GIL	1	2	1.5	2	0	0	6.5	0.36
GUN	2.5	3	0	0	1	2	8.5	0.47
IRL	1	3	2	3	2	2	13	0.72
JAM	1.5	0	1	2	0	0.5	5	0.28
KUR	2.5	3	3	3	3	2	16.5	0.92
MIN	1	0.5	0	0.5	0	1	3	0.17
SAN	1	3	3	3	0	1.5	11.5	0.64
TIR	2.5	2	3	3	2	3	15.5	0.86

Horizontal Inequalities (ECONHU, SOCHU)

Horizontal inequalities exist when the autonomous group is significantly better or worse off than other relevant social groups in the country, in particular the majority population, over a longer period of time. As has been argued, the analysis focuses on the economic (ECONHU) and social inequality dimension (SOCHU) in the consolidation phase. Cases of relative privilege are coded in the same way as cases of relative deprivation, because both may cause a deep sense of injustice. As argued above, the perception of inequality is fundamentally based on the actual living conditions of an ethnic group. Therefore, only objectively existing inequalities are considered. The conventional indicators for measuring economic inequality such as income, assets, or employment data serve as orientation for ECONHU. The assessment of SOCHU is based on the access to local health care facilities and the general health situation for group members. As further indicators, access to educational institutions and the general level of education are considered for the social dimension. For calibration, regional qualitative or quantitative data from national or regional statistical offices, United Nations, World Bank, or OECD databases are taken into account. The following case reports give a short overview of the calibration of the fuzzy scores for ECONHU and SOCHU.

Aceh

Aceh is an enclave economy from which the Acehnese do not profit. In fact, the regional income is well below the national average and the poverty rate clearly exceeds that of Indonesia. Despite relatively high education and health spending, there are significant differences in overall life expectancy and child mortality. This mainly affects the ethnic rural population, whose access to health facilities and medical staff is much more limited.

Åland

Åland's employment rate and disposable household income are above the average, but at a similar level to that in the capital region in the industrialized south of Finland. There are no differences between the Finns, the Swedes, and the Ålanders in terms of the social dimension either.

Atlantic Regions

The poverty rate of the indigenous peoples in the Atlantic Regions is significantly higher than that of non-indigenous peoples. Access to sanitation and health facilities is much more difficult for the ethnic groups in the region. The autonomous region is well below the national average in terms of both the literacy rate and the average duration of schooling in primary and secondary schools.

Basque Country

Per capita income and employment rate in the Basque Country are about one-third above the national average. However, as the differences to other prosperous regions inhabited mainly by the majority population are relatively small, economic inequalities are considered moderate. Economic prosperity ensures a well-equipped education and health system. Life expectancy in the autonomous region is the highest nationwide.

Bodoland

The region is considered one of the poorest in the country with strong economic and social disparities between the ethnic Bodo and the other groups in the state of Assam. The average annual income and literacy rate in a Bodo village are significantly below the state averages. More than 70 percent of the Bodos live below the poverty line.

Bougainville

Although Papua New Guinea is still one of the most underdeveloped countries, there are only weak asymmetries between the ethnic groups. As the average income in the autonomous region is slightly below the national average, economic inequalities are classified as "very weak". There are no significant differences in child mortality rates or general access to health care. The literacy and secondary school dropout rate is similarly high.

Catalonia

Catalans are a privileged group and thus a member of the ECONHU set. While the unemployment rate in recent years has been only slightly below the national average, there are clear disparities in household incomes and employment rates. On the social dimension, there are horizontal inequalities of low severity. Infant mortality is lower and life expectancy slightly higher. There are no significant differences on the educational dimension.

Chittagong Hill Tracts

The majority of Jummas survive on subsistence farming and are unable to generate monetary income. More than 70 percent of the indigenous population suffers from food shortages, that is, more than twice as many as in the central state. The child mortality rate is also well above the national average. About half of the inhabitants of the Hill Tracts have not received any education, compared to the national average of about 8 percent.

Corsica

The Corse unemployment rate has historically been well above the French average. The gross regional product (GRP) and the available household income per capita are well below the national averages. However, there are no significant differences on the social dimension.

Gagauzia

In one of the poorest countries in Europe, there are no significant horizontal inequalities between the Moldovan majority population and the ethnic Gagauz. The standard of living of both groups can be considered equal, taking into account all relevant indicators. There are also no differences in access to education and health care. The number of hospital beds and doctor visits per capita and the child mortality rate are similar to those in other regions.

Gilgit-Baltistan

Despite its exposed location only moderate inequalities prevail between the local population and the dominant group. Per capita income is about one-third below the national average, while the local poverty rate is slightly higher. On the social level, weak asymmetries can be identified on the basis of the chosen indicators. These exist mainly in the health sector. There are significantly fewer hospitals and sanitation facilities in the autonomous region. Child mortality is also slightly above the national average.

Guna Yala

The poverty rate in Guna Yala is about 30 percent above the national average. The income of non-indigenous peoples in Panama is, on average, more than three times higher than that of indigenous peoples. Access to basic health care is severely limited for the Kuna population. The proportion of malnourished infants is by far the highest in the country. The proportion of people without any educational attainment is significantly higher among members of the ethnic groups.

Jammu and Kashmir

There are significant economic disparities between Kashmiri Muslims and other groups in the region, including Hindus, Sikhs, Dards, and Ladakhis. The backwardness of the region also affects the socio-economic dimension. The literacy rate among Muslim Kashmiris is significantly lower than among Hindus or other groups in the region. However, there are no significant differences in the health dimension. Child mortality and life expectancy are more or less on par.

Kurdistan

The Kurds are relatively privileged compared to the Sunni and Shiite Arabs in the resource-rich region, when considering the poverty and unemployment rates or purchasing power, for example. Horizontal inequalities can also be identified on the social level. However, these appear to be somehow weaker than the economic disparities. The literacy and school enrollment rates in Kurdistan are considerably higher than those in Iraq.

Mindanao
The poverty rate in Mindanao is the highest in the country and is nearly 20 percent above the national average. In no other region of the country are medical facilities so rare as in the autonomous part of Indonesia. The proportion of those without any form of education is highest among the Moro nationwide. Also indicators such the number of school years or the proportion of graduates illustrate the severe social inequalities.

New Caledonia
The rate of unemployment among the Kanak is about four times higher than among non-Kanaks. Incomes are well below the average and many live under precarious conditions without access to running water, electricity, and sanitation. The Kanak are also systematically disadvantaged in education. Despite a comparatively well-equipped health care system, rates for child mortality, tuberculosis, and suicides are much higher among the ethnic Kanak.

Northern Ireland
Some moderate economic disadvantages for Catholics still exist. For example, the proportion of those who depend on state income support is significantly higher among Catholics, who also have a higher unemployment rate and a slightly lower average household income. In contrast, the once strong social inequalities between the two groups are no longer detectable. There are no group differences in access to health care or disparities in the duration of schooling or dropout rates.

South Tyrol
The employment rate and the annual household income in the autonomous region are significantly above the national averages. However, the disparities are due to the economic north-south divide of the country. The average income in the regions of northern Italy is lower than in South Tyrol, but is at a generally comparable level. There are no significant economic horizontal inequalities within the autonomous region. The same applies to school dropout rates or university enrollment rates. With regard to life expectancy and access to health facilities, no intergroup differences can be identified either.

Zanzibar

There are no significant group-related economic disparities between the Muslim-dominated autonomous island and the Tanzanian mainland. The proportion of those in the top income quintiles is slightly higher, but comparable to that in the capital region. The social dimension is calibrated with a fuzzy score of 0.2, as the supply of clean drinking water and access to sanitation are significantly better than in the rest of the country. There are no significant differences in the education infrastructure or literacy rate, the average duration of schooling, or dropout rates (Table 3.4).

Democracy (DEMO)

According to the theoretical arguments presented in Chap. 2, continuous democratization is expected to be a necessary condition for autonomy success. The condition is met when the democratic quality of the central state institutions improves shortly after the introduction of autonomy reforms and no major autocratization trend is observable in the subsequent period.

Table 3.4 Fuzzy scores for ECONHU and SOCHU

Case	*Economic inequalities*	*Fuzzy score ECONHU*	*Social inequalities*	*Fuzzy score SOCHU*
ACH	Very strong	1	Very weak	0.2
ALA	Non-existent	0	Non-existent	0
ATL	Very strong	1	Very strong	1
BAS	Moderate	0.7	Moderate	0.7
BOD	Very strong	1	Very strong	1
BOU	Very weak	0.2	Non-existent	0
CAT	Moderate	0.6	Very weak	0.3
CHT	Very strong	1	Very strong	1
COR	Moderate	0.6	Non-existent	0
GAG	Non-existent	0	Non-existent	0
GIL	Moderate	0.7	Very weak	0.3
GUN	Moderate	0.7	Strong	0.8
JAM	Moderate	0.7	Moderate	0.6
KUR	Very strong	1	Strong	0.8
MIN	Very strong	1	Very strong	1
CAL	Very strong	1	Very strong	1
IRL	Moderate	0.7	Non-existent	0
TIR	Non-existent	0	Non-existent	0
SAN	Non-existent	0.2	Very weak	0.2

Table 3.5 Fuzzy scores for DEMO

Case	*V-DEM value*	*After 5 years*	*After 15 years*	*After 30 years*	*Fuzzy score*
ACH	0.47	0.02	0.019	–	0.2
ALA	0.62	−0.004	−0.031	0.223	0.8
ATL	0.2	0.354	−0.063	−0.237	0.2
BAS, CAT	0.78	0.122	−0.001	0.01	1
BOD, JAM	0.57	0.43	0.012	−0.17	0.6
BOU	0.32	−0.003	−0.001	−0.315	0
CAL, COR	0.86	0.005	0.017	–	1
CHT	0.33	−0.052	−0.039	–	0
GAG	0.37	0.047	−0.091	–	0.55
GIL	0.34	0.013	–	–	0
GUN	0.22	0.004	−0.085	−0.063	0.4
IRL	0.78	0.048	0.075	–	1
KUR	0.3	−0.002	−0.021	0.002	0
MIN	0.49	−0.028	−0.096	–	0
SAN	0.3	−0.04	−0.004	0.087	0.4
TIR	0.56	0.022	0.031	0.028	1

Note: The V-DEM liberal democracy value is the democracy score at the time the autonomous region was established

For the analysis the V-DEM liberal democracy score is used, which fits the broad conceptualization of democracy and which is available for all consolidation phases.[7] From an empirical point of view, a case is a member of the DEMO set only if the values of the index have increased continuously since implementation. For orientation, three measurement points are set after five, 15, and 30 years. The five-year period serves to determine whether a rapid democratization took place. The periods of 15 and 30 years serve as a comparative description of the long-term development. With a score of 0.5 and higher, a country is considered more democratic than non-democratic (Table 3.5).

Engagement of International Organizations (ORGA)

Conciliations and consultations are the weakest forms of international participation and imply a more passive role of international actors. In contrast, international organizations play a more active role in mediation, arbitration,

[7] V-Dem Institute, "V-Dem. Varieties of Democracy. Global Standards, Local Knowledge"; Lindberg, "Ordinal Versions of V-Dem's Indices: For Classification, Description, Sequencing Analysis and Other Purposes."

and peace-keeping. While international mediation is primarily about finding an interest-based compromise between rival parties, arbitration results in a binding judgment of a decision-making authority. The most far-reaching form and highest level of intervention is peace-keeping, in which an organization provides military personnel to monitor an agreement. Table 3.6 gives a detailed overview of the form of international engagement in the respective cases and the fuzzy values assigned.

International Integration (INTEG)

International organizations encompass all organically structured, policy-related international regimes as well as regional, international, or

Table 3.6 Fuzzy scores for ORGA

Case	*Actors*	*Form of Intervention*	*Fuzzy score*
ACH	European Union, ASEAN, Crisis Management Initiative	Mediation	0.8
ALA	League of Nations, Sweden, United Kingdom	Conciliation	0.9
ATL	United Nations	Conciliation	0.6
BAS	*No international participation*		0
BOD	*No international participation*		0
BOU	United Nations; Australia, New Zealand, Fiji, Vanuatu; Peace Monitoring Group	Peace-keeping	1
CAL	*No international participation*		0
CAT	*No international participation*		0
CHT	India	Indirect (third state)	0.1
COR	*No international participation*		0
GAG	OSCE, Council of Europe	Consultation	0.6
GIL	*No international participation*		0
GUN	USA	Mediation (third state)	0.6
IRL	United States, European Union, Independent International Commission on Decommissioning, NGOs	Mediation	0.8
JAM	United Nations	Indirect Participation International Organization	0.3
KUR	*No international participation*		0
MIN	Organization of the Islamic Conference, European Union	Peace-keeping	1
SAN	No international participation		0
TIR	United Nations, Austria, United Kingdom	Consultation	0.7

Table 3.7 Fuzzy scores for INTEG

Case	*Criteria*				*Fuzzy score*
	Years until first membership	*Full membership*	*Memberships in total*	*Parallel memberships*	
ACH	–	1	2	1	0.6
ALA	48	2	4	4	0.9
ATL	–	–	–	–	0
BAS	13	6	11	3	1
BOD	–	–	–	–	0
BOU	–	–	–	–	0.1
CAL	2	4	7	2	0.9
CAT	25	7	10	4	1
CHT	16	1	2	1	0.4
COR	2	2	4	2	0.9
GAG	–	0	2	1	0.6
GIL	–	1	2	1	0.4
GUN	–	–	–	–	0
IRL	0	3	3	3	0.9
JAM	–	–	–	–	0
KUR	21	1	1	0	0.6
MIN	–	0	1	1	0.3
SAN	39	2	7	3	0.8
TIR	9	4	6	4	1

supranational institutions that are based on commonly agreed principles, rules, and norms. Four criteria are considered in order to calibrate the international integration (INTEG) condition: the duration until the first admission of an autonomous region, the kind of membership, the number of memberships in total, and the number of parallel memberships, that is, the central government is a member in the same organization as the regional government. A further distinction is made between partial memberships and full memberships. A partial membership implies cooperation with member states or possession of an observer status, but a lack of decision-making rights or veto power. Table 3.7 gives an overview of the international integration of the autonomous regions and the fuzzy values assigned.

Empirical Analysis

A systematic cross-case comparison of the calibration results with the outcome values indicates that most of the hypotheses are met. In fact, most successful cases were preceded by a non-violent conflict. On the other hand, there is no instance of autonomy failure after a non-violent conflict. At the same time, in all failed cases, ethnic movements have chosen some form of violent strategy. There is, however, no clear pattern when looking at the strategic goals of self-determination movements. Previous autonomy and secession goals can be found in both successful and failed cases. The rate of autonomy demands is even slightly higher among the failed cases.

Ninety percent of failed cases show strong and persistent horizontal inequalities between majorities and minorities. This applies to both the economic and the social dimension and corresponds exactly to theoretical expectations. The same is true for the regime type. Ninety percent of the successful autonomies are found in democratic or continuously democratizing central states. With regard to the failed cases, the share is only 44.4 percent. This, too, largely corresponds to the theoretical expectations (Table 3.8).

In 60 percent of successful cases, international organizations were involved in the process of post-conflict institutional engineering. However, there was no engagement of international organizations in the majority of failed cases. While 80 percent of successful autonomies have been integrated internationally, a large part of the failed cases are not integrated in international or regional networks. So, while there is indeed evidence for the theoretical considerations, it is the task now to determine whether the

Table 3.8 Calibration results and theoretical expectations

			Theoretical expectations
Successful autonomies			
Demands	10% Autonomy	90% Secession	Not met
Intensity	40% Non-violent	60% Violent	Not met
Economic Inequality	30% Not existent	70% Existent	Not met
Social Inequality	50% Not existent	50% Existent	(Not met)
Democracy	90% Democr.	10% No democr.	Met
International Organizations	60% Orga.	40% No orga.	Met
International Integration	80% Integ.	20% No integ.	Met
Failed autonomies			
Demands	77.8% Secession	22.2% Autonomy	Met
Intensity	100% Violent	0% Non-violent	Met
Economic Inequality	88.9% Existent	11.1% Not existent	Met
Social Inequality	88.9% Existent	11.1% Not existent	Met
Democracy	55.6% No democr.	44.4% Democr.	(Met)
International Organizations	66.7% No orga.	33.3% Orga.	Met
International Integration	66.7% No integ.	33.3% Integ.	Met

individual conditions, or combinations of conditions, reach the status of necessity or sufficiency. This is clarified in the following section.

Analysis of Autonomy Success

As mentioned above, a condition is necessary, if, whenever the outcome is present, the condition is also present ($x \leftarrow y$).[8] In terms of set relations, a necessary condition X is a superset of the Outcome Y, which means that each case's fuzzy-set membership score in X must be equal to or bigger than its membership in Y ($x \geq y$). The analysis of necessity shows that none of the identified conditions reaches the conventional consistency level 0.9 in either its presence or absence.[9] However, SCOPE nearly crosses the bar with a consistency score of 0.840. Only two deviant cases, Corsica and Guna Yala, contradict the statement of necessity (Fig. 3.1). SCOPE can therefore be deemed a quasi-necessary condition as almost all successful autonomies show a high degree of self-determination.

In order to test for sufficiency, the so-called truth table is logically minimized.[10] The intermediate solution allows for the designation of the treatment of logical remainders based on the theoretical assumptions made above. The procedure leads to the following solution formula: SCOPE∗DEMO∗INTEG → OUT, which unravels the basic and sufficient cornerstones of successful ethnic self-government: a high degree of transferred competencies, the establishment of autonomy in a democratic or

[8] In the following, the established QCA terminology is used to avoid conceptual ambiguity. Therefore, the terms "condition" (not independent variable) and "outcome" (not dependent variables) are used. If a condition consists of several conditions (conjunction, term) and connected with the logical AND, it is denoted with the symbol "∗" or written together (A∗B or AB). To describe logical alternatives (disjunctions, A+B), the symbol "+" is used. If several paths are combined by logical OR, I refer to this as a "solution". For the logical NOT (complement), the non-occurrence of a condition, the symbol "~" or lower-case characters are used (~A or a). The symbol "←" is used to describe necessity, "→" is used for sufficiency. I use the software R with the QCA package in version 3.3 (Dusa 2019) for the empirical analysis. The script can be downloaded from the following website www.felix-schulte.de/data.

[9] To sort out trivial necessary conditions, only factors with a coverage value higher 0.65 are selected. See Appendix for details.

[10] See technical appendix for details. The threshold value for consistency is set at 0.75 as the conventional benchmark.

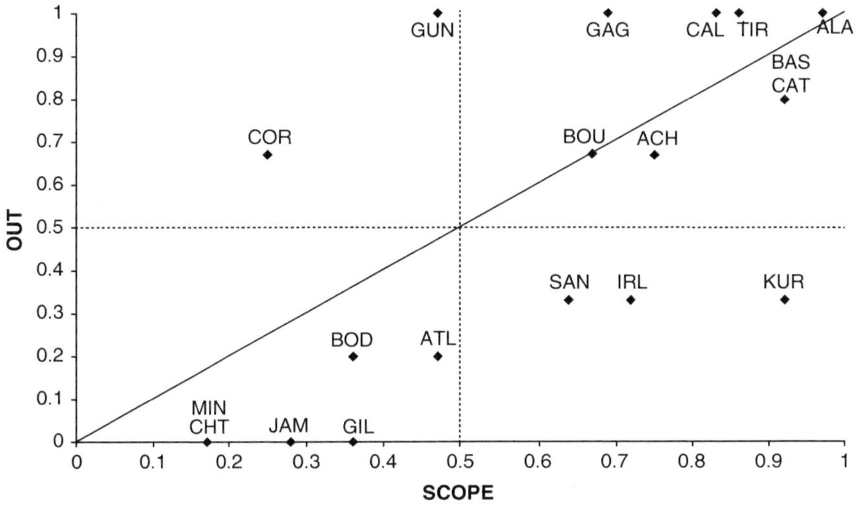

Fig. 3.1 XY-plot of SCOPE and OUT. (*Source*: Own illustration)

rapidly democratizing central state, and the international integration of the autonomy system.[11]

The solution formula has a raw coverage of 0.575 and covers 80 percent of the successful cases and 20 percent of the partly successful cases. A combination of SCOPE, DEMO, and INTEG already provides a comprehensive explanation for post-conflict autonomy consolidation in the European regions ALA, BAS, CAL, GAG, and TIR. The exclusion of logical remainders also provides information about the other conditions but yields a much more complex result (Table 3.9). These findings highlight the fact that autonomy consolidation as an extremely complex phenomenon can only be explained comprehensively by an interplay of specific structural and actor-centered factors.

Autonomy arrangements can apparently regulate even escalated self-determination conflicts, only if a high degree of autonomy rights was transferred and the institutional reforms received substantial international backing, either in the form of the participation of an international organization or in the form of a subsequent international integration of the

[11] Intermediate Solution with a Consistency of 0.891, Coverage of 0.575, and the Cases ALA, BAS, Cal, GAG, and TIR.

Table 3.9 Conservative solution for OUT

	Consistency	*Coverage*	*Cases*
stragy*scope*ECONHU*sochu*DEMO*orga *INTEG	1.000	0.116	COR
stragy*SCOPE*econhu* sochu *demo*ORGA*integ	0.819	0.127	BOU
stragy*SCOPE*econhu*sochu*demo*ORGA* INTEG	1.000	0.070	ACH
stragy*SCOPE*ECONHU*SOCHU*DEMO *orga*INTEG	1.000	0.160	BAS, CAL
STRAGY*SCOPE*econhu*sochu*DEMO*O RGA*INTEG	1.000	0.215	ALA, GAG, TIR
STRAGY*SCOPE*ECONHU*sochu*DEMO *orga*INTEG	1.000	0.135	CAT

region. Corsica is again a deviant case, which, however, was established in a full democratic central state (DEMO) and received a considerable degree of international integration (INTEG) in the consolidation period. Democratic environments are obviously important for cooperation processes and seem, to an extent, to compensate for other missing conditions. Contrary to the theoretical expectations, group inequalities can also be found in the solution terms for success. However, economic and social inequalities occur together only in one solution term. Whether these are remnants from the pre-autonomy phase and whether they have weakened in the consolidation phase need to be examined in further case studies. All solution formulas for OUT contain either the condition ORGA or the condition INTEG, which underlines the high importance of the international level for the peaceful regulation of ethnic conflicts.

The hypothesis H_1, claiming a peaceful and non-secessionist strategy is a key prerequisite for autonomy success, cannot be confirmed. Some successful cases with a violent conflict history contradict the theoretical assumption. It is not yet possible to make a clear statement about the empirical role of the two inequality dimensions. ECONHU and SOCHU appear in the conservative solution in their presence and absence, and in the intermediate solution, the conditions are entirely absent. This requires some further examination. The conditions are therefore included in the general model. Whereas ORGA is part of the solution formulas for the two outliers ACH and BOU, the second internationalization condition (INTEG) appears in various solution terms. Overall, internationalization appears to be a pivotal condition for autonomy consolidation. However, it seems that it can be achieved in various ways—either through international participation in the implementation period or via an international integration in the consolidation phase. This condition is therefore also included in the overall model.

Analysis of Autonomy Failure

The test on necessity reveals that, again, no single condition is a subset in its presence or absence for autonomy failure (out). The highest consistency score is achieved by ECONHU (0.844) and stragy (0.878), which both nearly reach the status of necessary conditions. Almost all failed autonomies show high and persistent economic inequalities between majority and minority or have seen a violent conflict beforehand. In each case only one deviating region, Zanzibar and the Atlantic coast, contradicts the statement of necessity. The logical minimization process of the truth table provides a rather complex picture. Post-conflict autonomy arrangements can obviously die in different ways. However, a closer inspection of the intermediate solution reveals that the theoretical expectations also hold true here[12] (Table 3.10).

A combination of violent secessionist conflict and strong inequalities contributes to autonomy reforms failing when there is no international

Table 3.10 Intermediate solution for out

	Consistency	*Coverage*	*Cases*
stragy*SCOPE*ECONHU*sochu*DEMO	0.845	0.200	IRL
stragy*ECONHU*SOCHU*demo*orga	0.881	0.352	CHT, KUR
stragy*scope*ECONHU*demo*orga*integ	0.896	0.287	GIL, CHT
stragy*scope*ECONHU*SOCHU*demo*integ	0.909	0.331	CHT, MIN
stragy*scope*ECONHU*SOCHU*orga*integ	0.872	0.302	CHT, BOD, JAM

[12] See Appendix for details. For the intermediate solution, we expected that the absence of STRAGY, SCOPE, DEMO, ORGA, and INTEG, and the presence of ECONHU and SOCHU are relevant for out. The most parsimonious solution, which includes all logical remainders in the minimization process that make the solution formula less complex, provides too complex results and is not very useful from an empirical point of view.

support and pressure on the conflicting parties to abide by agreements. Moreover, the failed cases CHT, KUR, GIL, and MIN are regions in undemocratic surroundings and have received a comparatively low degree of self-rule. IRL is a special case in this regard. Despite the high degree of autonomy and it being located in a fully democratic central state, post-conflict institutional reforms are considered to have failed at least partly due to the ongoing latent crisis and demands for secession. Here, too, rather strong group asymmetries, a high degree of preceding conflict intensity, and a lack of international support can be observed. In all terms, strong economic inequalities are part of the solution formula. The cases CHT, KUR, MIN, BOD, and JAM also show strong social inequalities.

The absence of recognition-enabling factors in combination with grievance-producing group inequalities lead to ongoing secessionist aspirations and, consequently, to the failure of conflict-regulating autonomy solutions. The set-theoretical analysis has shown that certain favorable and unfavorable, structural as well as actor-centered conditions for autonomy consolidation can be detected. The empirical results obtained so far can be summarized as follows: a high degree of self-rule, a democratic central state, international support, and absent group asymmetries are sufficient to autonomy success, whereas strong horizontal inequalities, violent and secessionist campaigns, an inadequate degree of autonomy, and low degrees of democracy and internationalization contribute to autonomy failure.

However, the results of the two initial QCAs reveal two empirical shortcomings that make it difficult to test the established theoretical models. On the one hand, the solution formulas are rather complex and cover relatively few cases. On the other hand, statements about the interplay of structural and actor-centered conditions, especially for failed cases, remain rather vague. In order to address these weaknesses, all tested conditions that are part of one of the solution formulas presented above in their presence or absence, and thus show some empirical relevance, are combined into two general models of autonomy success and failure. Wherever it makes sense, the individual conditions are then logically summarized to higher-order concepts to reduce the complexity of the resulting solution formulas. The empirical complexity can also simply stem from the fact that decisive explanatory factors were overlooked. The existing literature on post-conflict institutional engineering discusses other structural and actor-centered variables such as parties or electoral rules that may also have a decisive impact on the three-stage process of ethnic recognition. Their theoretical relevance is outlined in the next section. In a second step, the two overall models are enriched with these complementary conditions in order to provide a comprehensive and in-depth explanation for autonomy consolidation.

Complementary Factors

Consociational literature shows that democratic-inclusive institutions, in particular, are capable of overcoming deep cultural cleavages between identity groups. While all democracies offer some form of cooperation opportunities, those equipped with inclusive institutions are in a better position to do so. This, in turn, increases the likelihood of autonomy consolidation. The central and most important opportunity for citizens to influence politics is through elections. The electoral rules decide how votes are translated into mandates, regulate access to political power, and ultimately determine who rules and who does not. Majority voting systems with their inherent principle of "the winner takes it all" emphasize group differences rather than level them and trigger ethnic competition and thus prevent interethnic cooperation and moderate policies. Ethnic minorities, which are normally numerically smaller, remain politically marginalized even in the case of relatively concentrated settlement when the electoral system is based on majority voting. This may produce grievances and cause counter-reactions. By contrast, proportional representation systems (PR) are designed to have adequate group representation. Since the seats in the legislature are distributed according to the ratio of votes, smaller ethnic parties also have the ability to gain political influence. PR electoral systems thus prevent political marginalization and interethnic polarization. The frequent need for coalition governments creates incentives for cooperation and limits the concentration of power of a dominant majority. A proportional electoral system enables influence and opportunities for cooperation between elites at the central state level and is thus important for the second step of the postulated mechanism. The condition of the existence of a proportional voting system in the central state (PROP) is calibrated dichotomously based on the Electoral System Design Database.[13] For calibration, the electoral system of the central state for national parliamentary elections is taken into account. All voting systems belonging to the family of pro-

[13] IDEA, "IDEA. Electoral System Design Database."

portional voting systems are coded with a fuzzy score of 1. Electoral systems belonging to the majority voting systems are calibrated with the value 0.

Decentralization (DECEN) limits the power capacity of the dominant majority, increases participation opportunities at the regional level, and facilitates the overcoming of group boundaries through cooperation incentives and the mutual interdependence of different state levels. A decentralized central state has overcome, or never fully implemented, the model of a homogeneous nation-state and has institutionalized the recognition of different regional identities. If the power of the central government is already institutionally limited and there is a tradition of strong regions, this will have a positive effect on consolidation of autonomy as a special regional status, since not only are there more opportunities for cooperation, but attempts for recentralization are much less likely to occur. As the scope of regional fiscal and budgetary powers is, as described above, a suitable indicator of the autonomous capacity of a sub-state entity, the condition DECEN is calibrated on the basis of the Fiscal Decentralization Index using the method of direct calibration.[14]

While these institutions allow for political inclusion in a more or less direct way, the rule of law (RULE) is a more fundamental prerequisite. It is the rule of law that protects minority rights from the tyranny of the majority and allows for the legal recognition of ethnic identity. Only when governmental powers are bound by a legal system and fundamental human rights are part of this legal system can the recognition of cultural identity succeed in the long term. The condition RULE is calibrated on the basis of the Rule of Law Index.[15]

As argued, policy positions and the strategic orientation of political parties play a key role for actor behavior and elite preferences. While moderately left-wing, conservative, or liberal parties often support multiculturalism for reasons of social justice or winning ethnic voters, nationalist or right-wing authoritarian parties (NATIO) take anti-immigrant and anti-multicultural policy positions and promote power concentration, cultural homogeneity, and dominance of the titular nation. Such parties negatively influence other parties on the cultural policy dimension and have a polarizing effect on group relations. This hampers cooperation and rapprochement at the political level and, in the worst case, leads to renewed

[14] Ivanyna and Shah, "How Close Is Your Government to Its People?"

[15] World Justice Project, "WJP Rule of Law Index 2016 | The World Justice Project."

mobilization and conflict re-escalation in a consolidation phase. The condition NATIO is present when one or more nationalist parties have governed or have participated in a governing coalition in the central state over the past 20 years. The dichotomous condition is calibrated using the Political Institutions dataset.[16]

Another actor-specific factor, which has gained increasing attention in the research field in recent years, is the role of diaspora groups (transborder ethnic kin, TEK) and thus the transnational dimension of self-determination conflicts. Research points to TEK as being an important catalyst providing moral and logistical support beyond the direct reach of the central authorities. This increases the risk of conflict and the probability of separatist demands. It is assumed that transborder ethnic kin groups impede the consolidation of an autonomy solution, as such an agreement provides little benefit to diaspora groups or kin states. Diasporas will primarily favor independence, which brings with it full political and cultural dominance and an enlarged zone of influence for an ethnic community. It is assumed that a group considers an autonomy offer as inappropriate and insufficient and maintains secessionist claims if it is provided with external ideological and material support. Ongoing external support for a self-determination movement is particularly likely when the diaspora group itself is marginalized and hopes for a successful secessionist conflict or the respective group is under constant political pressure and experiences instrumentalization attempts by a patronage state. The condition TEK describes whether a group equipped with a special status belonging to the sample has one or more diaspora groups. It is calibrated using the Transborder Ethnic Kin dataset.[17]

As many autonomy critics have argued, the implementation of territorial autonomy provokes separatist desires among other ethnic groups in the country and generates a domino effect of ethnic unrest. When self-government is achieved by force, other groups believe that the use of violence is a promising strategy. Fearing disintegration and the collapse of the state, the central government reacts with repression and centralization. Although the argument is widely used in the literature, and often shapes political discourse in countries with breakaway regions, empirical results

[16] Cruz, Keefer, and Scartascini, "The Database of Political Institutions 2015 (DPI 2015)."
[17] Vogt et al., "Integrating Data on Ethnicity, Geography, and Conflict."

Table 3.11 Complementary factors

Complementary institutionalist conditions		
Proportional electoral system in central state (PROP)	Decentralization in central state (DECEN)	Rule of Law in central state (RULE)
Complementary actor-centered conditions		
Nationalist party in central state (NATIO)	Diaspora groups (TEK)	Ethnically homogeneous central state (HOMOG)

remain ambiguous.[18] In line with these research efforts, the condition of an ethnically homogeneous central state (HOMOG) is included in the actor-specific model. While territorial self-government is successful in central states with few relevant groups, because there are no rivals who might challenge the central government with similar demands, a permanent empowerment is unlikely in ethnically heterogeneous states, as central governments try to discourage other groups from making secessionist demands in the future. The condition is indirectly calibrated on the basis of the absolute number of relevant ethnic groups within the central state (Table 3.11).

Applying again fsQCA with the complementary conditions, we find that all successful cases exist in central states with PR electoral systems or decentralized state structures.[19] PROP + DECEN reaches a consistency score of 0.910 and a coverage of 0.660. Supplemented by rule of law, these factors are even sufficient to explain autonomy success. The combination RULE∗DECEN∗PROP → OUT reaches a consistency value of 0.787 and a coverage of 0.369. In contrast, neither NATIO, HOMOG, or TEK is a necessary condition in their presence or absence for autonomy success. The high importance of proportional systems is also evident in the analysis of autonomy failure as prop → out is sufficient for autonomy failure (Consistency = 0.644; Coverage = 0.649). The set-theoretical examination with the complementary factors shows clearly that the rule of law, inclusive state institutions such as decentralization and proportional voting, as well as the existence of nationalist parties must not be disregarded when explaining success or failure of post-conflict autonomy reforms and need to be included in the general models.

[18] Walter, *Reputation and Civil War*; Forsberg, "Do Ethnic Dominoes Fall?"; Toft, *The Geography of Ethnic Violence*.

[19] The detailed data values can be found in the Appendix.

General Models of Autonomy Success and Failure

To provide a reliable explanation for autonomy success and failure, all factors identified as empirically relevant in the previous QCAs are now merged into two general empirical models. This approach allows a most comprehensive explanation of the outcomes but has a serious weakness: the more conditions that are examined, the higher the probability of logical remainders. Since the number of factors studied significantly increases the number of logically possible configurations, solution formulas become again highly complex to interpret. Over-complexity can be avoided if there is a balanced ratio between the number of cases and the number of conditions. The present study follows the upper conventional limit in order to provide a robust explanation and to find evidence for the causal effect of single conditions on the three-stage process of ethnic recognition. A pragmatic solution to deal with many potential explanatory factors is to summarize different conditions based on theoretical considerations and to interpret them as higher-order concepts. This approach allows for a reduction of the logically possible configurations without losing too much information.

The rule of law is an undeniable component of liberal democracy. The conditions DEMO and RULE are therefore logically added to the condition "democratic constitutional state" (DEMOCR). A case is a member of DEMOCR if the central state is both a democracy and a constitutional state. INTEG and ORGA are based on the theoretical argument that autonomy consolidation and peaceful ethnic coexistence require external support from international actors. The condition INTERN describes the internationalization of the institutional reforms, whether through the involvement of international organizations in the implementation process or later through the integration of the region in international or regional networks.[20] The two inequality conditions ECONHU and SOCHU are combined in the same way and form the condition INEQU. The condition INEQU now describes whether strong economic or social inequalities exist between the ethnic groups. Again, the highest fuzzy score of the two original conditions gives the fuzzy value of the higher-order concept. PROP and DECEN were identified as empirically relevant in the institutional model. Both factors can be summarized on the basis of the theoretical

[20] The conditions are linked by a logical OR. According to the maximum rule, the highest fuzzy value of INTEG or ORGA gives the fuzzy value for INTERN.

considerations to a condition of "inclusive state organizations" (INCL). However, as it is very common in the sample that a central state has either a proportional representation or a decentralized state structure, the condition becomes trivial. As a proxy for inclusive state organizations, the condition PROP is used instead of combining the two conditions with Boolean algebra. However, additional robustness tests are performed with DECEN. The conditions SCOPE, STRAGY, and NATIO cannot be further summarized. Since a critical number of conditions have already been reached, TEK is excluded from the general model of success due to its rather low empirical relevance.

Based on the results of the previous QCAs, the respective conditions can now be assigned in their presence or absence. According to the assumptions, a combination of low inequalities, a high scope of autonomy, democracy, inclusive institutions, non-nationalist actors, and the engagement of international organizations or the international integration of the sub-state entity is sufficient for autonomy success (Fig. 3.2).

All factors identified for being important for autonomy failure are also merged into a holistic empirical model. This applies to persistent horizontal inequalities, a secessionist conflict strategy, a low scope of self-rule as well as exclusive state institutions. The existence of an anti-multicultural party, the lack of democracy and the rule of law, and the absence of international support are, as mentioned, not sufficient to explain autonomy failure. However, since these conditions have been conjunctural factors in various solution formulas, they are included in the empirical model (Fig. 3.3).

A sufficiency test confirms both empirical models. Except for natio, all conditions of the empirical model of success are found in the form of

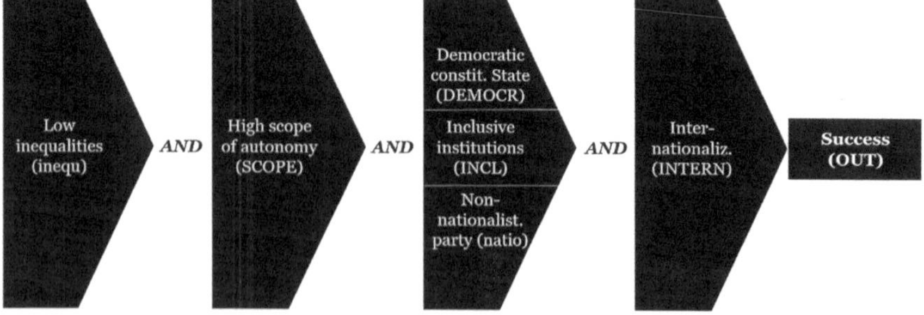

Fig. 3.2 Empirical model of autonomy success. (*Source*: Own illustration)

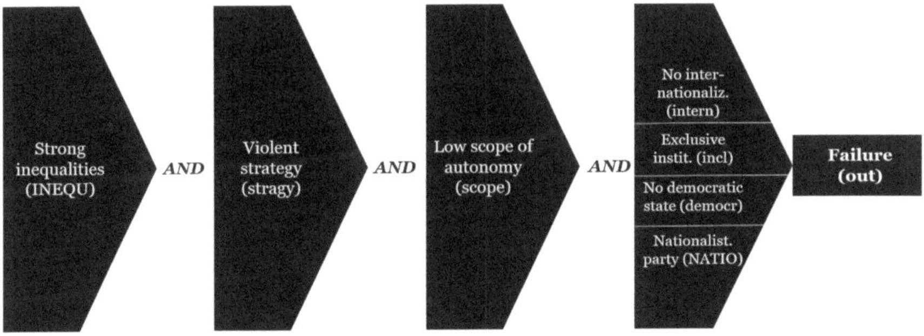

Fig. 3.3 Empirical model of autonomy failure. (*Source*: Own illustration)

Table 3.12 Results for the general models

	Cons.	*Cov.*	*Cases*
Model of success (conservative solution)			
SCOPE∗DEMOCR∗INCL∗natio∗INTERN	0.842	0.670	ALA, GAG, TIR, ACH, BAS, CAT, CAL
inequ∗SCOPE∗DEMOCR∗INCL∗natio∗INTERN	0.910	0.302	ALA, GAG, TIR
Model of failure (conservative and intermediate solution)			
INEQU∗stragy∗scope∗incl	0.905	0.464	BOD, CHT; GIL, JAM, COR, MIN

Note: Displayed are results with a consistency threshold of 0.9. The empirical role of NATIO, intern, and democr for out can also be demonstrated when separately including the factors into the set-theoretical analysis (see Appendix for details)

logical conjunctions. Most successful cases of the sample are covered by the solution formulas. In particular, the success of the European cases of territorial autonomy is well explained. CAT and BAS are two deviant cases with consistency in degree, whereas there is no case with consistency in kind (Table 3.12).

The basic solution formula for autonomy failure also provides a comprehensive explanation for five of the failed cases (BOD, CHT, GIL, JAM, MIN). Four failed cases are not covered by the term (ATL, IRL, KUR, SAN), but do not contradict the statement of sufficiency. COR is a deviant case with consistency in kind (Figs. 3.4 and 3.5).

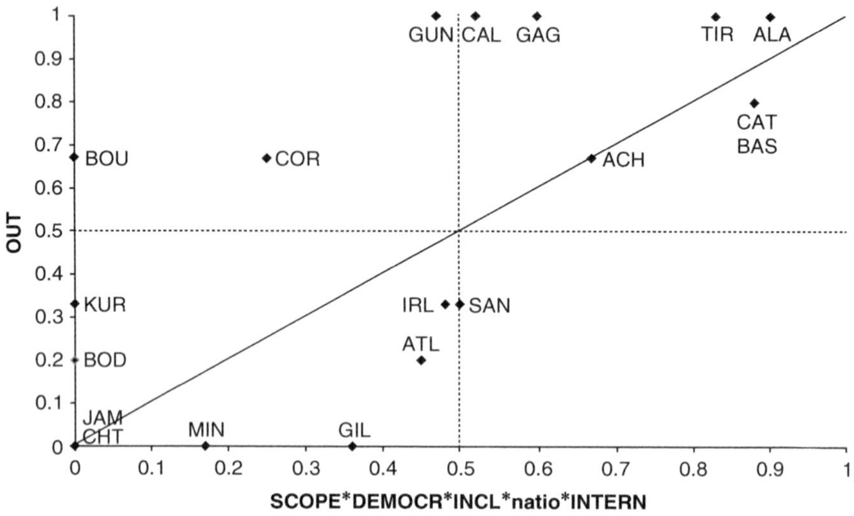

Fig. 3.4 XY-plot for the model of success. (*Source*: Own illustration)

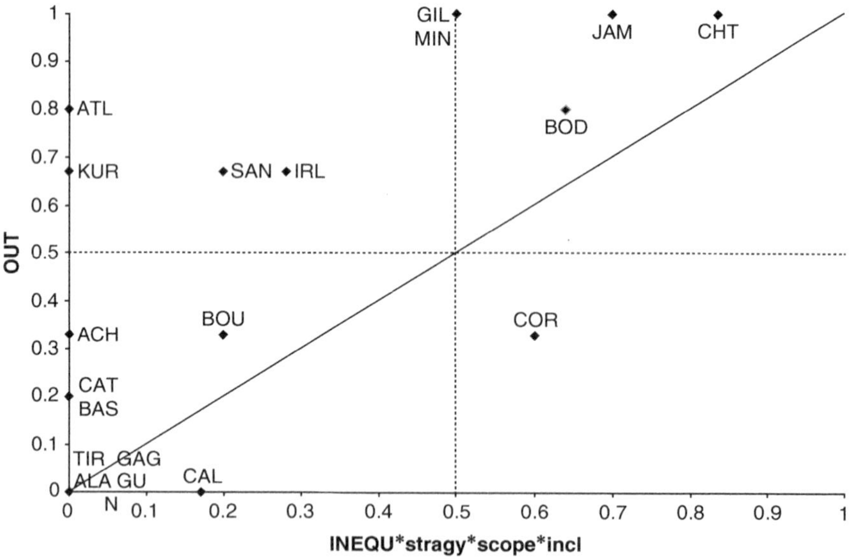

Fig. 3.5 XY-plot for the model of failure. (*Source*: Own illustration)

Robustness

The results hold against various robustness tests. On the one hand, the conservative, parsimonious, and intermediate solution formulas deliver almost identical results, which underlines the importance of the identified factor combinations for explaining the phenomena. On the other hand, the raw consistency thresholds were varied in the logical minimization process, which does not produce any deviating results. The strongest robustness test, however, is a test with other data. Therefore, in a first round, the calibration of the outcome condition is varied, whereby the success of an autonomy agreement now hinges on whether a violent domestic conflict has taken place after the implementation of post-conflict institutional reforms in the respective region.

On the basis of the UCDP armed conflict dataset, a three-value fuzzy set is constructed, differentiating between the absence of a violent conflict (fuzzy score 1), minor conflicts with between 25 and 999 battle-related deaths in a particular year (fuzzy score 0.33), and domestic wars with at least 1,000 battle-related deaths (fuzzy score 0).[21] Again, all solution formulas with different threshold values are explored. The results of the sufficiency test show that the empirical model remains valid against a different success measurement. The conservative and intermediate solutions with a consistency threshold of 0.8 exactly reflect the elaborated model. Due to the "harder" conflict measurement involving only highly violent conflicts, however, the number of successful cases drops to seven (ALA, CAL, CAT, COR, GAG, GUN, TIR) and includes only European autonomies with only one exception, GUN. In all other cases, violent ethnic conflicts with at least 25 deaths occurred during the consolidation phase. As a result, none of the solution formulas achieves a coverage score greater than 0.425, which means that the alternative measurement of the outcome delivers no broader explanation and cannot explain more cases of the sample. The empirical model for the negated outcome is also generally confirmed by the alternative measurement and provides a robust explanation for the typical failed cases.

In a second robustness test, I use other data both for the measurement of the outcome and for the conditions of the two empirical models. To

[21] Pettersson and Eck, "Organized Violence, 1989–2017."

calibrate OUT, I use data from the US military-based Integrated Crisis Early Warning System (ICEWS) project, which creates event data from automated content analysis of textual media information of international, regional, national, and local sources.[22] ICEWS collects all activities both between and within states and important actors and then classifies these activities on the basis of CAMEO (Conflict and Mediation Event Observations), on whether these events involve cooperative or hostile activities.[23] Based on the number of relevant non-cooperative events between the central governments and ethnic insurgents in the years 2015, 2016, and 2017, I assess the "restlessness level" of the specific region as a proxy for autonomy success. The 38,371 events found in the autonomous regions of the sample are assigned to five intensity levels on the basis of the CAMEO coding. As the calibration threshold for membership in OUT, I set a maximum of less than ten events of the highest intensity level (5) within the three-year period. The fine gradations within the set result first from the number of events at levels three and four, which also contain destructive actions, and second from the number of cooperative actions (level 1 and 2) within the given region. This assessment of the current social climate in the regions leads to 12 successful cases and seven failed cases and thus to slightly different results for OUT than the previous calibrations.

CHT, KUR, BOD, MIN, and JAM are clearly non-members of the set with several hundred events of the two highest conflict intensity levels. CHT, IRL, and this time also CAT fall out of the set due to ongoing secessionist movements and reported clashes between state forces and separatists. All other cases of the sample are members of OUT, whereas only ALA, GUN, and GAG show no level 4 and 5 events within the three-year period. The calibration of the conflict strategy (STRAGY) is now conducted on the basis of the SDM dataset, which provides information on whether a self-determination movement has used violence to achieve its goals.[24] The total number of years in which separatist violence occurred in the respective region between 1945 and the implementation of the institutional reforms is considered. The alternative

[22] Boschee et al., "ICEWS Coded Event Data."

[23] Schrodt, "CAMEO Conflict and Mediation Event Observations Event and Actor Codebook."

[24] Sambanis, Germann, and Schädel, "SDM."

calibration for DEMOCR is based on a measurement of the average level of liberal democracy of the central state. I use the combined Freedom House rating that consists of political rights and civil liberties.[25] Annual average scores are calculated from the year of the implementation of the autonomy system until 2017. In cases where the Freedom House data do not cover the entire consolidation phase, the values from year 1972 onward are used. The V-DEM variable "power distributed by social group" provides a comprehensive measurement of the inclusiveness of a political system and represents a suitable alternative to the purely institutional variables of a PR electoral system or decentralization to calibrate INCL. The variable takes values between 0 (political power is monopolized by one social group) and 4 (all social groups have roughly equal political power). Here, too, average scores are calculated for the respective central states in the consolidation phase.[26] Due to the lack of adequate data to measure horizontal inequalities between ethnic groups and the population majorities for all cases of the sample, I use the Gini index as a standard tool in the literature to calibrate INEQU.[27] Although it is a measure for vertical and not horizontal inequality, Gini scores may serve as a proxy for an unequal society.[28] For this second test I use the direct method of calibration. With this procedure, only the qualitative specification of the full membership of a case in the set and the full non-membership, as well as the indifference point, is necessary. The fuzzy values are then determined automatically using logarithmic functions placed between the qualitative anchor points. This requires fewer human calibration decisions and is an adequate alternative to the primarily theory-based indirect calibration method used in the previous QCA tests.

Also, this robustness test produces the expected results and confirms the empirical model. In particular, the conjunction of a high degree of autonomy (SCOPE), political inclusion (INCL), and international support (INTERN) remain the centerpiece of all success formulas. The

[25] Freedom House, "Freedom in the World. Country Scores."

[26] Pemstein et al., "The V-Dem Measurement Model."

[27] UNU-WIDER and V-DEM, "UNU-WIDER."

[28] Gilgit-Baltistan (GIL) is excluded from the analysis as data are not available for all conditions in this case. The calibration for NATIO is carried out as before on the basis of the Political Institutions Database. Since there are also no adequate alternative data for SCOPE and INTERN, I use the fuzzy scores from the previous model for these two conditions.

democratic nature of the central state (DEMOCR) and the absence of anti-multicultural parties are likewise components of most success paths. However, the analysis with different thresholds gives a more complex picture than the previous analyses. This is obviously due to the data choices that include broader indicators and lead to more blurred memberships. It is noticeable that a low degree of inequality plays a role in only a few formulas. This can also be attributed to the calibration of the condition using the Gini index. In contrast, a peaceful and non-secessionist self-determination movement is found much more frequently as a decisive factor for later success in autonomy, as initially assumed. The stated explanation for autonomy failures is also confirmed by the testing with alternative data. All identified conditions appear within the predicted presence or absence. The conservative solution including logical remainders provides the term INEQU∗stragy∗scope∗incl∗internal∗NATIO → out (consistency = 1; coverage = 0.214), and exactly reflects the empirical model.

Appendix

Table 3.13 Summary of calibration scores

CASE	*STRAGY*	*SCOPE*	*ECONHU*	*SOCHU*	*INEQU*	*DEMO*	*ORGA*	*INTEG*	*INHAB*	*KIN*	*TEK*	*REGIO*
ACH	0	0.75	1	0.2	1	0.2	0.8	0.6	0.1	0	0	1
ALA	0.9	0.97	0	0	0	0.8	0.9	0.9	1	1	0	0
ATL	0.7	0.47	1	1	1	0.2	0.6	0	0.7	0	1	1
BAS	0.4	0.92	0.7	0.7	0.7	1	0	1	0.3	0	1	0
BOD	0.2	0.36	1	1	1	0.6	0	0	0.3	0	0	1
BOU	0.2	0.67	0.2	0	0.2	0	1	0.1	0.9	1	0	0
CAL	0.4	0.83	1	1	1	1	0	0.9	0.8	0	0	0
CAT	0.8	0.92	0.6	0.3	0.6	1	0	1	0	0	0	0
CHT	0.1	0.17	1	1	1	0	0.1	0.4	0.6	0	0	1
COR	0.4	0.25	0.6	0	0.6	1	0	0.9	0.8	0	0	0
GAG	0.7	0.69	0	0	0	0.55	0.6	0.6	0.9	0	0	1
GIL	0.3	0.36	0.7	0.3	0.7	0	0	0.4	0.4	0	1	1
GUN	0.7	0.47	0.7	0.8	0.8	0.4	0.6	0	1	0	0	1
IRL	0.2	0.72	0.7	0	0.7	1	0.8	0.9	0.4	1	1	0
JAM	0	0.28	0.7	0.6	0.7	0.6	0.3	0	0	1	1	1
KUR	0	0.92	1	0.8	1	0	0	0.6	0.1	0	1	1
MIN	0.2	0.17	1	1	1	0	1	0.3	0.2	0	0	0
SAN	0.2	0.64	0	0.2	0.2	0.4	0	0.8	0.9	0	1	1
TIR	0.6	0.86	0	0	0	1	0.7	1	0.7	1	1	0

(*continued*)

Table 3.13 (continued)

CASE	*HOMOG*	*DEMOCR*	*RULE*	*DECEN*	*INCL*	*PART*	*NATIO*	*PARLA*	*PROP*	*INTERN*	*OUT*
ACH	0	0.67	0.6	0.5	1	1	0	0	1	0.8	0.67
ALA	1	0.9	1	0.76	1	1	0	1	1	0.9	1
ATL	0.67	0.45	0.2	0.16	1	0	0	0	1	0.6	0.2
BAS	0.33	0.88	0.75	0.74	1	1	0	1	1	1	0.8
BOD	0	0.69	0.55	0.48	0.48	1	1	1	0	0	0.2
BOU	1	0.43	0.3	0.14	0.14	0	1	1	0	1	0.67
CAL	0.67	0.95	0.1	0.75	1	1	0	0.5	0	0.9	1
CAT	0.33	0.88	0.6	0.74	1	1	0	1	1	1	0.8
CHT	0.67	0.43	0.75	0.45	0.45	0	1	1	0	0.4	0
COR	0.67	0.95	0.9	0.75	0.75	1	0	0.5	0	0.9	0.67
GAG	0.67	0.67	0.2	0.18	1	0	0	0.5	1	0.6	1
GIL	0.33	0.41	0.8	0.5	0.48	0	0	1	0.5	0.4	0
GUN	0.33	0.77	0.4	0.2	1	0	0	0	1	0.6	1
IRL	0.33	0.96	0.55	0.52	0.48	1	0	1	0	0.9	0.33
JAM	0	0.69	0.1	0.48	0.48	1	1	1	0	0.3	0
KUR	1	0.4	0.55	0.06	1	1	1	1	1	0.6	0.33
MIN	0.67	0.6	0.8	0.5	0.75	0	0	0	0.5	1	0
SAN	0.33	0.5	0.3	0.21	0.75	0	0	0	0	0.8	0.33
TIR	0.33	0.87	0.7	0.49	0.52	1	0	1	1	1	1

Analysis of Autonomy Success

Table 3.14 Test on necessity

Condition	*Consistency*	*Coverage*
STRAGY	0.590	0.843
stragy	0.583	0.486
SCOPE	0.840	0.736
scope	0.368	0.485
ECONHU	0.553	0.465
econhu	0.570	0.803
SOCHU	0.393	0.442
sochu	0.707	0.700
DEMO	0.728	0.747
demo	0.365	0.395
ORGA	0.467	0.631
orga	0.593	0.511
INTEG	0.736	0.708
integ	0.380	0.442

Note: Test for single conditions for OUT with a minimal consistency threshold of 0.9

Table 3.15 General test on necessity for OUT

	Consistency	*RoN*	*Coverage*
SCOPE+econhu	0.903	0.646	0.719
SCOPE+sochu	0.930	0.523	0.668
SCOPE+DEMO	0.913	0.559	0.677
SCOPE+INTEG	0.903	0.584	0.685
sochu+DEMO	0.927	0.586	0.697
STRAGY+econhu+INTEG	0.953	0.560	0.696
STRAGY+sochu+INTEG	0.960	0.479	0.662
econhu+DEMO+INTEG	0.933	0.527	0.671

Table 3.16 Truth table for OUT

	STRAGY	*SCOPE*	*ECONHU*	*SOCHU*	*DEMO*	*ORGA*	*INTEG*	*OUT*	*N*	*Cons.*	*Cases*
1	1	1	0	0	1	1	1	1	3	1.0	ALA, GAG, TIR
2	0	1	1	1	1	0	1	1	2	1.0	BAS, CAL
3	0	0	1	0	1	0	1	1	1	1.0	COR
4	0	1	1	0	0	1	1	1	1	1.0	ACH
5	1	1	1	0	1	0	1	1	1	1.0	CAT
6	0	1	0	0	0	1	0	1	1	0.819	BOU
7	0	1	1	0	1	1	1	0	1	0.589	IRL
8	0	1	0	0	0	0	1	0	0	0.562	SAN
9	1	0	1	1	0	1	0	0	2	0.537	ATL, GUN
10	0	0	1	1	1	0	0	0	2	0.500	BOD, JAM
11	0	1	1	1	0	0	1	0	1	0.417	KUR
12	0	0	1	1	0	0	0	0	1	0.380	CHT
13	0	0	1	1	0	1	0	0	1	0.368	MIN
14	0	0	1	0	0	0	0	0	1	0.324	GIL

Note: Displayed are only rows with empirical cases

Analysis of Autonomy Failure

Table 3.17 Test on necessity

Condition	*Consistency*	*Coverage*
STRAGY	0.314	0.404
stragy	0.878	0.658
SCOPE	0.567	0.447
scope	0.664	0.789
ECONHU	0.844	0.639
econhu	0.292	0.370
SOCHU	0.663	0.671
sochu	0.448	0.339
DEMO	0.378	0.349
demo	0.729	0.706
ORGA	0.370	0.450
orga	0.697	0.541
INTEG	0.467	0.404
integ	0.662	0.693

Note: Test for single conditions for out with a minimal consistency threshold of 0.9

Table 3.18 General test on necessity for out

	Consistency	*RoN*	*Coverage*
scope+demo+integ	0.922	0.603	0.661

Table 3.19 Truth table for out

	STRAGY	*SCOPE*	*ECONHU*	*SOCHU*	*DEMO*	*ORGA*	*INTEG*	*OUT*	*N*	*Cons.*	*Cases*
1	0	1	1	1	0	0	1	1	1	1.000	KUR
2	0	1	1	0	1	1	1	1	1	0.967	IRL
3	0	0	1	1	0	0	0	1	1	0.884	CHT
4	0	0	1	0	0	0	0	1	1	0.865	GIL
5	0	0	1	1	0	1	0	1	1	0.842	MIN
6	0	0	1	1	1	0	0	1	2	0.800	BOD, JAM
7	0	0	1	0	1	0	1	0	1	0.767	COR
8	0	1	0	0	0	0	1	0	1	0.692	SAN
9	1	1	1	0	1	0	1	0	1	0.630	CAT
10	0	1	1	0	0	1	1	0	1	0.614	ACH
11	1	0	1	1	0	1	0	0	2	0.610	ATL, GUN
12	0	1	0	0	0	1	0	0	1	0.394	BOU
13	0	1	1	1	1	0	1	0	2	0.375	BAS, KAL
14	1	1	0	0	1	1	1	0	3	0.093	ALA, GAG, TIR

Note: Displayed are only rows with empirical cases

References

Boschee, Elizabeth, Jennifer Lautenschlager, Sean O'Brien, Steve Shellman, and James Starz. "ICEWS Coded Event Data," 2018. https://dataverse.harvard.edu.

Cruz, Cesi, Philip Keefer, and Carlos Scartascini. "The Database of Political Institutions 2015 (DPI 2015)," 2016. http://publications.iadb.org.

Dusa, Adrian. *QCA with R. A Comprehensive Resource.* Berlin: Springer International, 2019.

Forsberg, Erika. "Do Ethnic Dominoes Fall? Evaluating Domino Effects of Granting Territorial Concessions to Separatist Groups." *International Studies Quarterly* 57, no. 2 (2013): 329–340.

Freedom House. "Freedom in the World. Country Scores," 2018. http://freedomhouse.org.

Harguindéguy, Jean-Baptiste Paul, Alistair Cole, and Romain Pasquier. "The Variety of Decentralization Indexes: A Review of the Literature." *Regional & Federal Studies* (2019): 1–24 (Online First). https://doi.org/10.1080/13597566.2019.1566126.

Hooghe, Liesbet, Gary Marks, and Arjan H. Schakel. *The Rise of Regional Authority: A Comparative Study of 42 Democracies.* London and New York: Routledge, 2010.

Hooghe, Liesbet, Arjan H. Schakel, Gary Marks, Sara Niedzwiecki, Sandra Chapman Osterkatz, and Sarah Shair-Rosenfield. *Measuring Regional Authority: A Postfunctionalist Theory of Governance.* Oxford: Oxford University Press, 2016.

IDEA. "IDEA. Electoral System Design Database," 2017. www.idea.int.

Ivanyna, Maksym, and Anwar Shah. "How Close Is Your Government to Its People? Worldwide Indicators on Localization and Decentralization." *Economics E-Journal* 8, no. 3 (2014): 1–64.

Ladner, Andreas, Nicolas Keuffer, and Harald Baldersheim. "Measuring Local Autonomy in 39 Countries (1990–2014)." *Regional & Federal Studies* 26, no. 3 (2016): 321–357.

Lindberg, Staffan I. "Ordinal Versions of V-Dem's Indices: For Classification, Description, Sequencing Analysis and Other Purposes." V-Dem Working Paper, no. 20, 2015. https://www.v-dem.net.

Pemstein, Daniel, Kyle L. Marquardt, Eitan Tzelgov, Yi-ting Wang, and Farhad Miri. "The V-Dem Measurement Model: Latent Variable Analysis for Cross-National and Cross-Temporal Expert-Coded Data." SSRN Scholarly Paper. Rochester, NY: Social Science Research Network, 2018. https://papers.ssrn.com.

Pettersson, Therése, and Kristine Eck. "Organized Violence, 1989–2017." *Journal of Peace Research* 55, no. 4 (2018): 535–547.

Sambanis, Nicholas, Micha Germann, and Andreas Schädel. "SDM: A New Data Set on Self-Determination Movements with an Application to the Reputational Theory of Conflict." *Journal of Conflict Resolution* 62, no. 3 (2017): 656–686.

Schrodt, Philip A. "CAMEO Conflict and Mediation Event Observations Event and Actor Codebook," 2012. http://data.gdeltproject.org.

Schulte, Felix. "The More, The Better? Assessing the Scope of Regional Autonomy as a Key Condition for Ethnic Conflict Regulation." *International Journal on Minority and Group Rights* 25, no. 1 (2018): 84–111.

Schulte, Felix, and Christoph Trinn. "Untangling Autonomy. Introducing the Territorial Self-Governance Dataset (TERRGO)." Paper presented at IPSA Colloquium Sarajevo, 2019.

Toft, Monica Duffy. *The Geography of Ethnic Violence: Identity, Interests, and the Indivisibility of Territory.* Princeton: Princeton University Press, 2010.

UNU-WIDER, and V-DEM. "World Income Inequality Database," 2017. https://www.wider.unu.edu/database/.

V-Dem Institute. "V-Dem. Varieties of Democracy. Global Standards, Local Knowledge," 2016. https://www.v-dem.net/en/.

Vogt, M., N.-C. Bormann, S. Ruegger, L.-E. Cederman, P. Hunziker, and L. Girardin. "Integrating Data on Ethnicity, Geography, and Conflict: The Ethnic Power Relations Data Set Family." *Journal of Conflict Resolution* 59, no. 7 (2015): 1327–1342.

Walter, Barbara F. *Reputation and Civil War: Why Separatist Conflicts Are so Violent.* Cambridge: Cambridge University Press, 2009.

World Justice Project. "WJP Rule of Law Index 2016. The World Justice Project," 2016. http://worldjusticeproject.org/rule-of-law-index.

CHAPTER 4

The Causal Mechanisms Behind Autonomy Success and Failure

Ethnic leaders accept autonomy reforms if these entail a high degree of self-determination and, therefore, political power. However, only if office-seeking political elites can rely on support from the masses, they will engage in further constructive cooperation with the central government and turn away from secessionist demands. Elites will only be supported, if large parts of the group recognize that territorial autonomy reforms improve their current situation and have a credible commitment that their special status and official recognition will endure in the future. Yet real empowerment only leads to a decline of collective deprivation and paves the way for public bargaining support for ethnic leaders if there are no grievance-producing inequalities prevailing between majority and minority in a post-conflict consolidation phase. The extremely difficult rapprochements between the national government and ethnic elites at the political level require adequate opportunities for ongoing cooperation, which are offered by democratically inclusive institutions. As has been argued above, both cooperative and minority-friendly parties in the central state as well as the support of international organizations contribute to the success of such elite cooperation, which then provides a fruitful basis for rapprochement processes between rival groups.

Accordingly, autonomies fail when ethnic elites oppose institutional reforms because of a too low degree of self-rule and persistent economic or social horizontal inequalities produce new grievances that are easily utilized for further mobilization by nationalist demagogues. This is all the

F. Schulte, *Peace through Self-Determination*, Federalism and Internal Conflicts,
https://doi.org/10.1007/978-3-030-37587-4_4

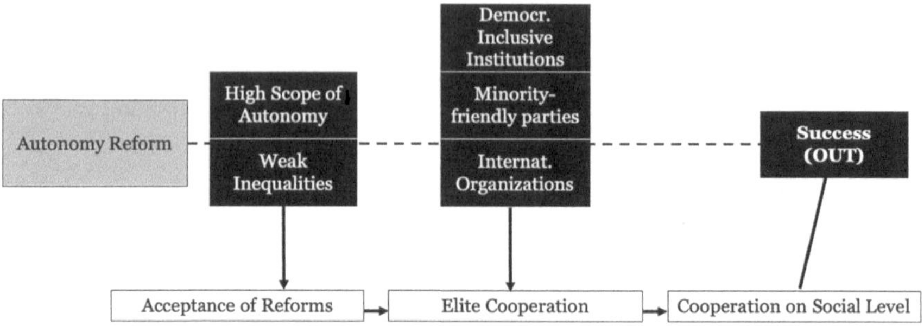

Fig. 4.1 Causal model of autonomy success. (*Source*: Own illustration)

easier when groups have previously fought each other in secessionist conflicts and nationalist and anti-multicultural parties in the central state are constantly accelerating the spiral of ethnic polarization that is hardly halted due to a lack of democracy, rule of law, and international support. The combination of the malus conditions initiates a triad of non-acceptance, grievances, and mobilization, and ultimately leads to the failure of post-conflict territorial autonomy. Combining these theoretical considerations with the two empirical models from the previous section gives the following two causal models (Figs. 4.1 and 4.2).

While it has already been shown that the identified conditions are individually necessary and, in their combination, jointly provide a sufficient explanation for autonomy success and failure, it now has to be demonstrated that the sets of factors have a causal influence on the process of ethnic recognition. If we find case-based evidence that these combinations of structural and actor-centered conditions have indeed caused the acceptance of reforms and cooperation respectively refusal, grievances, and mobilization, then the underlying theoretical argument of the study can be confirmed.

Process-tracing is a suitable empirical tool in order to detect whether the postulated causal mechanisms linking the conditions and the outcomes are actually present and whether they function as theoretically assumed. The ambition is now to go beyond identifying necessary and sufficient conditions and QCA as a rather static snapshot-method, but to uncover the causal mechanisms between the conditions and the outcome. In a

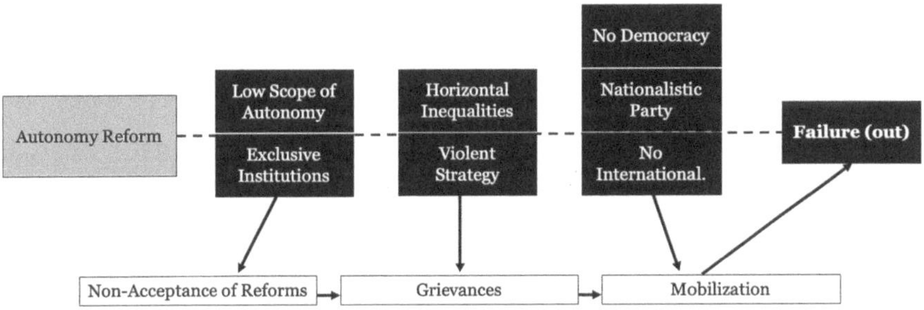

Fig. 4.2 Causal model of autonomy failure. (*Source*: Own illustration)

theory-testing analysis, it is advisable to study cases in which it is reasonable to assume that the particular mechanisms actually occur.[1]

For autonomy success we find three typical cases, which show high membership values in the success formula SCOPE∗DEMO∗INCL∗nation∗INTERN → OUT. These are Åland (ALA), South Tyrol (TIR), and Gagauzia (GAG). The representative case of South Tyrol (TIR) is particularly interesting for testing causal mechanisms, as it shows full membership in the outcome set, and in contrast to Åland (ALA) and Gagauzia (GAG), the South Tyrolean autonomy arrangement has successfully consolidated after a violent self-determination conflict. The case is thus empirically more relevant to illustrate the usefulness of the theoretical model than the other two representative cases of autonomy success. Typical cases of failed autonomy reforms are the Chittagong Hill Tracts (CHT), Jammu and Kashmir (JAM), and Bodoland (BOD). The case Chittagong Hill Tracts has the highest membership scores in the solution formula INEQU∗stragy∗scope∗incl → out and is therefore selected as the representative case for testing the causal model of autonomy failure.

In both cases, the diametrically opposed "one state, one nation, one people" claim of a hegemonic titular nation and demands for self-determination by a marginalized minority group escalated in the context of the (re-) establishment of a nation-state. In both cases, a peace treaty provided territorial self-governance and wide-ranging self-determination for the minority groups. Despite several crises, territorial self-governance

[1] Beach and Rohlfing, "Integrating Cross-Case Analyses and Process Tracing in Set-Theoretic Research," 14.

in South Tyrol has been successfully consolidated and continues to ensure a peaceful coexistence between Italians, Ladins, and South Tyroleans. After about two decades, the institutional reforms have led to broad mutual recognition at the societal level.

In contrast, territorial self-governance in the Chittagong Hill Tracts is still only partially implemented and has not peacefully settled ethnic tensions between the Bengali-dominated central government and the ethnic Jumma. To this day, violent clashes between ethnic rebels, state security forces, and paramilitary settler groups continue. The different outcomes of the post-conflict institutional reforms can be explained on the basis of the two causal models and the absence or presence of the identified conditions, supporting or preventing the three-stage process of mutual recognition.

Autonomy Success: The Case of South Tyrol

The historic passland between Germany and Italy was part of the Habsburg Empire since the fourteenth century and included both a German and an Italian speaking part. The area was divided as a result of the First World War and the German-speaking part south of the Brenner Pass was annexed to Italy. The Italian government, especially after the fascist victory, was eager to homogenize the region. From 1922 onward, the minority suffered from various repressive assimilation measures, such as the ban of the German language, the artificial introduction of Italian surnames and toponymy, and the state-supported mass migration of Italians. Their proportion in the region increased from about 4 percent in 1900 to about 25 percent in 1939.[2] The final step of the Italianization was an agreement ("option") between Hitler and Mussolini confronting the South Tyroleans with the choice between a forced resettlement to the German Reich and a compulsory assimilation within the Italian Empire. A large percentage of South Tyroleans decided to leave their ancestral land, although only a relatively small part of them actually left due to the outbreak of the Second World War. Euphoria surrounding the occupation of the area by German troops disappeared when repression continued, especially against the "Non-Optants". Dissatisfaction grew when the Paris Peace Treaty of 1946 made the region a part of Italy again, despite the historical affinity of the

[2] Marko, Palermo, and Woelk, *Tolerance through Law. Self Governance and Group Rights in South Tyrol.*

German-speaking South Tyroleans with Austria. While the demands for a referendum on the reintegration to Austria remained unheard, the Allies insisted on protective provisions for the South Tyroleans. This prompted Italian Prime Minister Alcide De Gasperi and Austrian Foreign Minister Karl Gruber to sign a bilateral treaty (Gruber-De-Gasperi Agreement) acknowledging Austria's role as a protective power and providing for special protection of the German-speaking minority and the establishment of a regional authority.

In 1948, the central government issued a first statute of autonomy, which, despite the bilateral agreement, did not entail real self-rule for the ethnic group as the government merged the German-speaking territory with the Trento region into a single province, leaving decision-making powers in the hands of the Italian majority. The interests of the South Tyroleans were easily outvoted as a result. However, Italy considered the obligations to be fulfilled by having established the Autonomous Region Trentino-Alto Adige/South Tyrol. When the repressive assimilation measures of the interwar period restarted, ethnic tensions escalated. After ever-growing rallies, the first bombs of the South Tyrol Liberation Committee (Befreiungsausschuss Südtirol, BAS) exploded at the end of the 1950s, followed by years of violent attacks, arbitrary arrests, curfews, and torture. During the course of the escalating conflict, the Austrian kin state turned to the United Nations. In reaction to international pressures, Italian Minister of the Interior, Mario Scelba, prevailed against internal resistance and set up the 19-Commission, consisting of 12 Italians, six Germans, and one Ladin, to work out a viable solution to the conflict. The inclusive commission presented a series of proposals for the establishment of territorial self-governance in April 1964, which were accepted by the two Foreign Ministers and Social Democrats, Guiseppe Saragat and Bruno Kreisky. Despite continued violent attacks, the parties agreed on a specific catalog of measures ("package") which marks the beginning of the consolidation phase.

Acceptance of the Autonomy Arrangement

After heated debates, the South Tyrolean People's Party (SVP), the mouthpiece of the German-speaking group, voted by a narrow majority at its party conference in November 1969 for the adoption of the deal. The moderate package-supporters among Governor Magnago resisted the party's radical-irredentist forces, whereas the high degree of proposed competencies played a pivotal role for the choices of the party elites. The argument of the advocates that "there will be no better offer" was ultimately much more convincing than the criticism of the opponents who could not make a realistic alternative proposal for the future of the minority within the Italian nation state. "What happens if we say no? No one was able to answer this question. I can tell you right now. The United Nations resolution enters into force (…). Then we will probably end up before the [International Court of Justice], as has already been said, without a package, because we said no (…). Now the rope is ripping. Bird eat or die! But when the bird eats, it lives, and otherwise it dies, that's the difference!"[3]

Magnago convinced the South Tyroleans, given the lack of realistic alternatives, to accept the package solution. The most convincing argument was that he could offer autonomy critics the possibility to exert influence in further negotiations with the Italian government. Despite the victory of the package proponents, a fundamental consensus for the institutional reforms grew among the SVP elites, who soon agreed with the Italian government on a schedule ("operations calendar") for implementing the package measures. By constitutional law, which came into force in January 1972, the mountainous region received its special status. In 1992, the Italian government announced to the Austrian government that the package has been fully implemented, and the latter issued an official declaration of dispute settlement to the United Nations.

The high degree of autonomy that was gradually becoming a reality for the South Tyroleans weakened the formerly dominant discourse of oppression. The wide-ranging competencies helped to regain control over the identity-forming territory with its resources and cultural symbols. The autonomous province took over welfare, housing, and the preservation of monuments and quickly worked on enacting the first laws for the protection of "their" flora and fauna. The perceptible decline in the feeling of deprivation paved the way for broad electoral support of the SVP under the leadership of charismatic Magnago, which achieved an average of 65 percent of the vote between 1956 and 1968.[4] Its bureaucratic handling of the autonomy policy left little room for conflict-prone symbolism and took the self-determination movement's revolutionary spirit. The BAS

[3] Zeitgeschichte Informationssystem, "22./23.11.1969: Auszug Der 18-Stunden-Debatte Der SVP-Landesversammlung in Meran," https://www.uibk.ac.at/zeitgeschichte/zis/library.

[4] Ferrandi, Pallaver, and Leonardi, *La regione Trentino-Alto Adige*, 636.

fighters, discredited by the political elite, were increasingly losing popular support. The articulation of suffering and the desire for reunification were soon replaced with a detailed discussion about the specific institutional setup, policy-making processes, and stronger domestic guarantees.

Starting in the mid-1970s, South Tyrol underwent a profound transformation that was brought about by the dynamic interplay of far-reaching self-government, democratization, economic upswing, and a profound change from materialist-authoritarian to more liberal values. This social change proved to be surprisingly robust against the turbulences that occurred, such as the polarizing language group survey in the 1981 census, the rise of the neo-fascist Movimento Sociale Italiano (MSI), and the new wave of violent separatist attacks in the 1980s. Although the package did not go far enough for many, the majority agreed with the pragmatic position of the SVP. It was found particularly positive that the now open public service offered well-paying jobs, of which the number increased from around 1,000 to over 5,500 between 1970 and 1980.[5] They brought the minority closer to the central state administration, which had previously been reserved for Italians and had been the origin of most repressive assimilation measures. The increased self-confidence was reflected in a decline in protests, and an increase in both political and economic activism and a slow change in public opinion, which was reflected in the then very popular addition of "I am a South Tyrolean" to the Italian license plate. This clearly showed that remaining in the central state and support for moderate policies was socially accepted, as the oversized "I" as identifying Italy immediately caught the eye of everyone.[6]

Elite Cooperation

"It is not enough to notice the emigration of our people and complain about it. We have to see with which measures we can defend ourselves as South Tyrolean. We have to take what we can take [...] unfortunately we are a minority, which was thrown into the sea in 1918. And when you're in the sea, you have to keep your head above water. [...] Our people want from us party leaders that we work with all our forces to make things change".[7] On the basis of the steadily growing acceptance of the package

[5] Solderer and Clementi, *Das 20. Jahrhundert in Südtirol. Autonomie Und Aufbruch*.
[6] Grote, *I Bin a Südtiroler*, 225.
[7] Own translation. Zeitgeschichte Informationssystem, "22./23.11.1969."

solution observed by SVP politician Roland Riz in 1969, a political and cultural opening of the group elites took place. These openings, as postulated by the theoretical model, have opened the doors for a constantly intensified cooperation at regional, national, and international levels.

Between its foundation after the Second World War and the end of the millennium, the SVP changed from an irredentist separatist party into a moderate-conservative regional party. Its strong ethnic "Volkstums"—ideology began to crumble after the first internal criticism ("Aufbau") in the 1960s, leading to deeper internal differentiation and a stronger focus on welfare policy. The ethnic cleavage, however, dictated the policy positions until the 1990s: "The political objective is to secure and promote the German and Ladin ethnic groups and to consolidate them as a majority in their traditional homeland", as stated in the 1993 manifesto.[8] Since the early 1990s, a more pragmatic leadership took over the party administration and gradually expanded the ideological corset. Since 1998, the SVP has formally advocated a "positive coexistence" with the Italian language group. That same year, the party successfully campaigned for Italian voters for the first time. Although the party still defines itself in terms of ethnicity, the SVP can no longer be programmatically distinguished from other conservative Christian Democratic parties, not least because the number of Italian voters is constantly growing.

The political-cultural opening of the SVP is a direct consequence of the party's continued electoral success. This electoral success is fundamentally based on a steady decline in the electorate's feeling of deprivation, which supported the party in its moderate course. The South Tyroleans began to realize that they benefited from the special status and endowed the party with an absolute majority between 1948 and 2008. The elites, for their part, refrained from mobilizing for unconventional politics. While until the 1960s, all regional parties shared the ideological positions of the SVP and agreed to the policy of ethnic separation, the era of center-left coalitions at the central state level, which began in 1963, heralded political change.

It was the center-left representatives who adopted pro-minority positions, particularly at provincial level, and thus initiated further rapprochement and reconciliation. In the mid-1970s, the New Left/Nuova Sinistra party, which was both programmatically and organizationally interethnically

[8] Südtiroler Volkspartei, "Das neue Programm Der Südtiroler Volkspartei beschlossen von Der Landesversammlung Am 8. Mai 1993" (SVP, Meran, 1993), www.svp.eu.

organized, took the final leap across the ethnic rubicon, and sent out the decisive signals to overcome the ethnic separation at the political level. On the basis of this political change, cooperation efforts between majority and minority representatives intensified within democratic-inclusive institutions and regional networks. A landmark institution was the aforementioned 19-Commission appointed by the Italian Council of Ministers under the leadership of Christian Democrat Mario Scelba and chaired by Social Democrat Paolo Rossi. This inclusive institution provided a suitable forum for negotiations and compromises based on the similar policy positions of the parties. After 1972, the cooperation was successfully maintained in mixed parliamentary commissions to develop implementing provisions. Former package-critics were integrated in these bodies minimizing the destructive potential of spoilers.

In the autonomous government, the SVP and the DC formed an enduring alliance that lasted from 1948 until 1993. While interethnic executive power sharing is a fundamental and legally entrenched principle of the 1972 autonomy statute, the continuity and crisis resistance of this coalition are nonetheless worth mentioning. Although the SVP left the regional government in Trento in the years of violent clashes, it did not take this step in the province of Bolzano and remained part of the actual autonomy government. After 1993, the SVP forged coalitions with the parties of the center-left alliance, Ulivo/Unione, in the course of its programmatic opening and political transformation toward a moderate conservative party. The high willingness of the actors to cooperate in the difficult first consolidation phase can be traced back to the similar policy positions rooted in Conservatism, Catholicism and anti-Communism, whereas the regional DC often mediated between the Roman DC and the SVP in difficult times.[9]

Despite the majority voting system introduced between 1993 and 2005, South Tyroleans were always able to send representatives to both chambers of the Italian Parliament. Continuous political inclusion largely mitigated the deep mistrust toward the central authorities to such an extent that the SVP transformed into an active legislative force on national level. After 1970, the party began to actively support the center-left coalitions, which can be understood to be a direct impact of growing cooperation on the sub-state level. At that time, national debates increasingly found their way into South Tyrolean politics and an increasing number of

[9] Pallaver, "South Tyrol's Changing Political System."

SVP statements on non-autonomy issues can be observed. In 2001, the party concluded an election agreement with the Italian center-left alliance, Ulivo. For the first time, SVP voters in the constituency of Bolzano supported an Italian candidate. Cooperation manifested and continued at the international level, particularly after the official settlement of the dispute in 1992 and the beginning era of European integration. As argued, the United Nations and Austria as a kin state and protecting power played a fundamental role in settling the conflict. While these two actors confined themselves to a rather passive watchdog role after the first few years, it was political integration in European and interregional networks that offered important possibilities not only for communication networks and economic promotion but also for gaining political significance and a form of "external recognition".

The SVP elites understood relatively early the high importance of European integration and supranationalism for the survival of South Tyrol's autonomy arrangement and the protection of their political and cultural rights. European affairs soon became an important alternate option to the demand for reintegration into the Austrian motherland. Within the Italian delegation to the European Union and within the European People's Party, the SVP began to build strong collaboration networks with central state parties such as the Unione di Centro and the Nuovo Centrodestra and used this mouthpiece to continuously "present its own situation" as the former Governor Luis Durnwalder put it.[10]

In addition, interregional cooperation helped to overcome the national borders that made the ethnic minority a minority in the first place. The autonomous government is included in various regional networks and plays an active part in the Committee of the Regions of the European Union, the Alps Working Community (Arge Alp) with the regions of Italy, Austria, Germany, and Switzerland, or within the cooperation network of the regional parliaments of Tyrol, Trentino, and Vorarlberg. The political borders between the territories of the historical Tyrol have thus become largely permeable. The international sphere and the integration of the region into international structures are considered a strong guarantee for the special status and, ultimately, the cultural survival of the ethnic group.

[10] Provincial Administration South Tyrol, "Alle News | Bereich | Landesverwaltung | Autonome Provinz Bozen - Südtirol."

Rapprochement on the Societal Level

Despite the ethnic division policy of the mono-ethnic SVP and group boundaries cemented by the declaration of language group affiliation, executive power sharing, and proportional representation, successful cooperation at the political level sent decisive signals for processes of rapprochement at the societal level. The constant willingness to compromise and the moderate policy positions of political elites stopped the spiral of polarization and mistrust. The elites emphasized the advantages of the special status for South Tyrol instead of repeating the historical injustice and group marginalization. These impulses paved the way to move closer together, at both the civil society and private sector levels, and, ultimately, to reorganize social relations from an "against each other" attitude in the 1970s to a largely peaceful "coexistence" in the 1990s and, eventually, to an emerging "togetherness" in the new millennium. In the first decades of the consolidation phase, group membership had confessional character and pluriethnic-oriented South Tyroleans were defamed as "gravediggers" of their own ethnic group.[11]

With the student movement of 1968, a slow and tenacious resistance against the cultural cleavage began. With Christian and peace-ethical arguments, students, intellectuals, and clergy tried to advance the rapprochement between South Tyroleans and Italians. Political activists such as Alexander Langer initiated an interethnic countermovement with projects such as the magazine *Die Brücke*, in which German and Italian articles were published regularly for the first time. A second driving factor was entrepreneurs in the border region who, for mainly economic reasons, were hardly interested in growth-inhibiting ideologies. Business Associations openly expressed the multi-ethnic character of the region and promoted the rapprochement of groups in the labor market.

However, disputes about the introduction of proportional representation in the public service, the allocation of social dwellings, and mandatory language tests forced the South Tyrolean society back into ethnic trench warfare between "Welsche" and "Crucchi". After the establishment of territorial self-government, it took almost a decade for the tense group relations to ease. While the obligatory proportional ethnic representation in government and administration as an integral part of the institutional reforms cemented the cultural cleavage between the language

[11] Zappe, *Das ethnische Zusammenleben in Südtirol*, 282.

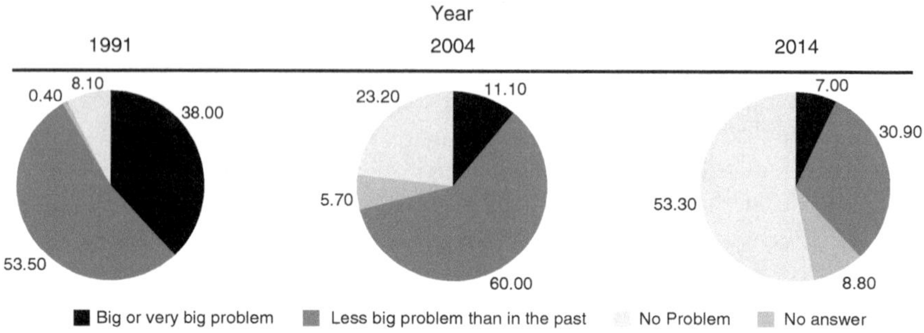

Fig. 4.3 Mutual recognition in South Tyrol. (*Note*: Percentage of answers to the question "How do you feel about the coexistence of the three ethnic groups in South Tyrol?" *Source*: Provincial Statistics Institute South Tyrol)

groups, the integrative institutions fostered the development of personal relationships, helped to dismantle prejudices and to build mutual trust. Both sides recognized that the special territorial status as well as its consociational design offered decisive advantages. Strong historic economic or social asymmetries between the language groups that would have hindered the social rapprochement process did, as mentioned above, not persist in the autonomy consolidation phase (Fig. 4.3).

While South Tyrolean society was characterized by a strong and exclusive group consciousness in the first two decades after the implementation of the regional autonomy system, the slow development of an overarching and interethnic regional identity can be observed in the course of the increasing lifespan of the autonomous region. By the mid-1980s, open confrontation and ethnic hate speech were no longer socially acceptable. The original dogma of the older generation of freedom fighters and the first SVP leadership, which can be described as "as little cooperation with Italian authorities as possible, as much as necessary", changed to "as much cooperation as possible, but not a complete overcoming of the group boundaries".

Today, it is still considered useful, often even pleasant, to speak the language of "the others" and to adopt their customs, habits, and food as well. At the same time, it is still tacitly accepted that there are insurmountable differences between the groups. Today, 97.6 percent of German-speaking teenagers still prefer to spend their time with peers from the same language group.[12] Although the society shows a strong verzuiling and parties, schools, kindergartens, and sports clubs are ethnically separated to this day, mutual recognition between groups as the basis for peaceful ethnic cohabitation has been achieved. In 1991, 38 percent of Italians, Germans, and Ladins found living together problematic. In 2004, the number dropped to 11.1 percent. Today, only 7 percent hold this opinion.[13] The proportion of those who describe the coexistence as positive, however, increased from around 8 percent in 1991 to 23.2 percent in 2004 and finally to 53.3 percent in 2014. As much as 35 percent of German speakers consider ethnic coexistence as unproblematic today. Among Italians, there are almost as many (34.8%) who agree. Secessionist parties, such as Die Freiheitlichen (DF) or the Süd-Tiroler Freiheit (STF), had so far not been able to initiate a strong separatist movement that could call on greater support. About 67.5 percent of South Tyroleans claim to have great confidence in the institutions of the autonomy system and are generally satisfied with public services.[14] Especially in recent years, a certain pride has developed in the special status of the region and the successful regulation of ethnic tensions. Against the background of the recent ethnic self-determination conflicts and independence referendums on the continent, politicians on both sides have repeatedly pointed to the "South Tyrolean Way".

Autonomy Failure: The Case of Chittagong Hill Tracts

The Chittagong Hill Tracts (CHT) in the remote southeast of Bangladesh are populated by several ethnic groups, most notably by the Chakma, Marma, and Tripura, which have developed an overarching cultural identity, known as Jumma, and share similarities in customs and social organization. They differ greatly from the Bengali majority population in terms of their religion, language, and traditions. With the beginning of British colonial rule over their settlement area, the traditional Jumma

[12] Provincial Statistics Institute South Tyrol, "Jugendstudie. Werthaltungen, Lebensformen und Lebensentwürfe der Südtiroler Jugend."

[13] Provincial Statistics Institute South Tyrol, "Südtiroler Sprachbarometer. Barometro Linguistico Dell'Alto Adige. Sprachgebrauch Und Sprachidentität in Südtirol"; Provincial Statistics Institute South Tyrol, "Schriftenreihe 211."

[14] Provincial Statistics Institute South Tyrol, "Astat Info."

self-government ended in the mid-eighteenth century. However, the administrative classification of the region as a "backward tract" allowed the ethnic group to retain at least some self-rule. This administrative division gradually lost its importance as the area fell to Pakistan in 1947 despite vehement protests by the Bengalis. The region became a poorly protected "tribal area" in the Islamic Republic and the traditional institutions were subordinated to the strongly centralized structures of the central state. The Jumma's dissatisfaction with their lost self-determination grew into a strong antagonism as since the 1950s more and more non-indigenous peoples migrated to the Hills and the central government increasingly exploited natural resources in the area. The Kaptai Dam, built in the early 1960s, rendered thousands of hectares of fertile land unusable ("Lake of Tears"), destroyed cultural sites, and displaced hundreds of thousands of people from their ancestral land.

After years of bitterness and alienation from Pakistan's political system, the Jumma leaders used the window of opportunity created by Bangladesh's founding in 1971 to reclaim their political autonomy. In February of the same year, a delegation led by Manabendra Narayan Larma met the Prime Minister of the ruling Awami League (AL), Sheikh Mujibur Rahman. The Jumma elites demanded the re-establishment of territorial self-government, the protection of the Jumma culture and their traditional institutions, and a ban on the migration of non-indigenous settlers to the region.[15] However, the head of government, also a dominant figure of the Bengali national movement, which had just reached the goal of a separate nation-state after a bloody war of secession, brusquely rejected the demands, but demanded the group's firm commitment to Bengali nationalism.

Shortly after the founding of the state, the central government began to put into practice Bengali hegemony in politics, business, and society. Part of the "one state, one nation, one people" policy of the ruling Awami League was, as in the case of South Tyrol, to change the demography of the ethnic settlement area through the targeted settlement of members of the majority population. The proportion of Bengalis in CHT increased from less than 2 percent in 1872 to more than 9 percent in 1959 and finally to about 50 percent in 1991.[16] Seeing their cultural survival in danger, the Jumma organized themselves under the leadership of Larma in the "Parbatya Chattagram Jana Samhati Samiti" (PCJSS). After further

[15] Achankeng, *Nationalism and Intra-State Conflicts in the Postcolonial World*, 322.
[16] Mohsin, *Conflict and Partition: Chittagong Hill Tracts, Bangladesh*, 23.

unsuccessful political efforts, an armed unit named the Shanti Bahini lent weight to the demands of ethnic self-determination. The central government reacted to first clashes with a complete militarization of the area. For their part, the Shanti Bahini succeeded in attracting more and more deprived men from remote hill villages to counter the military occupation with increasingly heavy guerrilla attacks on military facilities and Bengali settlements. The ethnic self-determination conflict escalated into a long and bloody civil war in which an estimated 8,500 civilians lost their lives.

Even after the formal return to parliamentarism, the subsequent central governments oriented their policies toward strong nationalism and Islamization and continued to consider the uprising as a mere security and development issue. After more than 20 years of protracted conflict, first peace talks with the PCJSS were opened in the mid-1990s, from which the "Chittagong Hill Tracts Peace Accord" emerged in December 1997. The agreement provides a special autonomy status for the provinces of Khagrachhari, Rangamati, and Bandarban. Regional bodies, the so-called Hill District Councils, were set to receive substantial executive and legislative powers, an independent commission is to settle upflaming land disputes, and state troops should be withdrawn except for a few military posts.[17] However, more than 20 years after the agreement on an autonomy reform, the conflict in the Chittagong Hill Tracts is still in a violent crisis and has expanded on an interethnic dimension between supporters and opponents of the 1997 peace agreement.

Non-acceptance of the Autonomy Arrangement and Continued Grievances

Already during the peace talks, there were large demonstrations against the institutional reforms in central Bangladesh, which several Bengali organizations, the BNP and the Jamaat-i-Islami movement among others, had called for. Also, the Jumma elites did not unanimously support the agreement. Criticism was expressed in particular in the student wing of the Jumma organization that the autonomy agreement would primarily benefit the Bengals: "The agreement […] clearly demonstrated the political bankruptcy of the PCJSS […]. Leaders of this party have compromised the people's interest and fallen deep into the marshland of opportunism. They have made it their raison d'être to advance self-interest by winning

[17] Chittagong Hill Tracts Accord, "Chittagong Hill Tracts Accord."

favor of the ruling party other than to carry the struggle forward for establishing people's rights".[18] Just a few months after the end of the peace talks, the opponents of the autonomy reforms organized in the United People's Democratic Front (UPDF), which has since torpedoed the implementation of the 1997 peace agreement. The UPDF complains that the degree of self-rule is inadequate; it calls for reserved seats in the national parliament, urges fixed quotas in educational institutions and national border guards, and demands constitutional protection of the special status. The autonomy reform is perceived as highly elitist, exclusive and being enforced by the Bengal majority.

Although the PCJSS, the dominant Jumma organization, basically supports the peace treaty, it also criticizes the incomplete implementation of the autonomy reforms and the lack of political inclusion in national decision-making processes. The initial optimism within the party was followed by disappointment at the turn of the millennium when the slow transfer of powers under AL rule came to an almost complete halt when the nationalist BNP gained power in 2001, regional elections were suspended, and the Constitutional Court declared the incompatibility of the regional institutional framework with the state constitution.

The dissatisfaction of the elites was widely shared among the masses as their daily lives did not improve in the consolidation phase due to ongoing ethnic marginalization. Group grievances are fueled by ongoing repression by the military or military-backed settler organizations in the form of abuses, especially against women and children, land grabbing and other economic and social discrimination, and limited freedom of movement and assembly: "[...] The Bengali settlers very often try to terrorize the tribals, they loot their crops, occupy their lands, rape their women, they dishonor any tribal they like [...]. But the offenders are never booked or punished. Some people of the law enforcing agencies are very often found encouraging the settlers in their nefarious activities and sometimes they themselves become involved".[19] (Fig. 4.4).

The nationalist central government, which shows no interest in multicultural policies and group empowerment, is held primarily responsible for the discrimination against the Jumma people. A majority of the group members simply saw no reason to endorse the peace treaty. More than half (51.9%) of the hill residents say that the autonomy agreement has not

[18] UPDF, "United Peoples Democratic Front Manifesto."

[19] Chakma, *Ethnic Cleansing in Chittagong Hill Tracts*, 141.

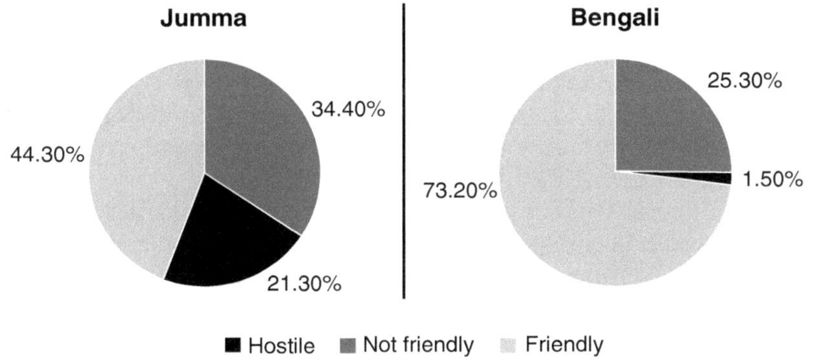

Fig. 4.4 Mutual non-recognition in CHT. (*Note*: Percentage of answers to the question "How do you feel about the coexistence of the ethnic groups in the Chittagong Hill Tracts?" *Source*: Barkat et al., 2008, 2009)

condemned violence in the region.[20] Over 55 percent of the Jumma describe the coexistence between the ethnic groups as "unfriendly" or even "hostile". About 81 percent of Jumma claim to have been threatened or blackmailed in the past.[21]

Mobilization and Collective Action

Persistent social and economic inequalities, continuing military repression, and ethnic discrimination created strong grievances among the group members which are repeatedly instrumentalized by ethnic leaders: "The back of the Jumma peoples has already touched the wall and that they are left with no space for a back march. This compels the Jumma peoples to take up tougher movement [...] the hills will burn unless the agreement is implemented in full".[22] The wheel of mobilization has never stopped running since the beginning of the conflict in the 1970s. It was initially powered by the UPDF at the beginning of the consolidation phase, but for some years now, the PCJSS has also been engaged in mobilization efforts. The renewed resort to a violent strategy appears to both Jumma

[20] Mohsin, *Conflict and Partition: Chittagong Hill Tracts, Bangladesh*, 41.

[21] Barkat et al., "Situation Analysis of Chittagong Hill Tracts in Bangladesh. An Analysis Based on 'Socio-Economic Baseline Survey of Chittagong Hill Tracts' Data."

[22] PCJSS, "UNPO: Chittagong Hill Tracts: PCJSS Statement on 20th Anniversary of CHT Accord (Jyotirindra Bodhipriya Larma)," 7.

organizations as the only way to achieve real empowerment and to restore a positive group identity. In order to illustrate the causal mechanism between ethnic marginalization, grievances, and collective action and to find evidence for the causal effect of the identified conditions, conflict events that occurred during a six-month period in the northern district of Khagrachari are exemplified below.[23]

In November 2016, ethnic protests broke out in the district after some Jumma drowned in the Mainee River due to the long-complained lack of a bridge. After ever-increasing student rallies in December 2016, the arrest of a UPDF activist triggered a wave of massive protests against ethnic discrimination and military rule in the province. The demonstrations are violently suppressed by state security forces, which prompted new counter-reactions by protesters. A group of gunmen attacked the local AL leader and devastated his office in Narikel Bagan. This was followed by a major protest march of several hundred AL supporters and Bengali settlers as well as house searches and arrests in Jumma villages by state forces in January 2017, to which indigenous protesters reacted with blockades and street riots. The unsolved murder of a Jumma student at the end of February and the police's ban on the indigenous Boisabi festival for alleged lack of permission fueled tensions, which re-escalated when the leader of UPDF-affiliated student organization Pahari Chhatra Parishad (PCP) died in captivity. The UPDF and the PCP both called for mass rallies and demanded an independent investigation of the death of the PCP leader, punishment of the military commander, and the withdrawal of the military according to the provisions of the CHT accord. In April, various settler groups blamed the Jumma for the murder of a Bengal teenager, whereupon PCP activists attacked a building of a newspaper, which was accused of having called the PCP leader a terrorist. In mid-May several Bengali settler groups announced a violent countermovement in Khagrachari district, which, possibly backed by the military, carried out various arson attacks on Jumma hill villages. A renewed mobilization of ethnic elites in response to these events further maintained the vicious circle of violence.

[23] Both the location and the date have been chosen arbitrarily to increase the robustness and to demonstrate the omnipresence of the social mechanism and the impact of the identified factors. The descriptions are based on a qualitative content analysis of newspaper articles by Dhaka Tribune, The Daily Star, One News BD, and Kaler Kantho as well as written statements by PCJSS, PCP, and UPDF, published between November 2016 and June 2017.

Remobilization is heavily boosted by the instable political environment and the anti-multicultural aspirations of the two dominant parties in the central state, the Awami League (AL) and the Bangladesh Nationalist Party (BNP). In the two decades since Ershad's downfall, power has alternated between the two parties and various non-party caretaker governments. Despite fierce and often violent competition, both parties share a strong commitment to an exclusive form of Bengali nationalism, an ideology, which is diametrically opposed to ethnic recognition and the full granting of territorial autonomy. Multicultural policies and ethnic empowerment are seen as a huge security threat and contradicting the idea of a powerful, unitary, and ethnically homogeneous Bengali nation-state.

The central state is a highly defective, non-consolidated democracy with a weak rule of law, high level of corruption, and restricted rights of freedom. The hyper-centralization of political power under the Westminster-style electoral and parliamentary system, the sharp political divide between AL and BNP, and the increasing influence of extremist Islamic organizations have fueled the political discourse and created a fragile and highly polarized institutional environment. Politics has become a zero-sum game. Riots after elections are common events and the military still plays a key role in political decision-making processes. Democratic freedoms are virtually non-existent for the Jumma. After the outbreak of the majority-minority conflict, as mentioned, the ethnic settlement territory became a heavily militarized area, with full control by the armed forces and no room for democratic participation and ethnic self-government. In the national parliament, the group is, except a few hand-picked PCJSS representatives, not represented and the sub-state institutions serve as controlling bodies of the central government and are dominated by Bengali representatives. This reduces the Jumma's ability to exert conventional political influence and prevents any rapprochement at the political level.

The international community took little notice of the peace treaty, let alone its implementation. No international organization was engaged in the consolidation phase in order to change the preferences of the actors toward peaceful cohabitation and political bargaining and limit their centrifugal actions. The spiral of polarization thus rotated unhindered. Bangladesh views the ethnic conflict as a purely domestic issue. The pressure of neighboring India on the PCJSS and the Shanti Bahini played a certain role for the entry of the Jumma elites into peace negotiations. In the consolidation phase after 1997, however, India did not take a role as an active patronage state, so as not to burden relations with the neighboring state. The central state, operating below the radar of the international community, felt little pressure to comply with the peace agreement and to fully implement the territorial autonomy arrangement. The Jumma felt left alone and ethnic organizations were barely prevented from taking up arms again. The counterfactual nature of this speculation notwithstanding, it is reasonable to assume that international peacekeepers might have had a positive influence on the actors and, consequently, could have reduced the conflict intensity to a more manageable level.

Summary

The South Tyrol case has demonstrated that a positive attitude of the ethnic elites toward institutional reforms was necessary to initiate cooperation efforts that could then be continued and intensified on the societal level. Only on this basis could a mutual recognition emerge, which forms the basis of the success of South Tyrol's territorial autonomy system today. The case study has shown that the high degree of self-rule provided by the package deal convinced the SVP elite and was the decisive argument for critics to support the institutional reforms. Real empowerment and the absence of horizontal inequalities made feelings of deprivation among group members gradually decrease. The group members were willing to support the elites in their policy of rapprochement. The continuous negotiation processes between the SVP and the Italian government were only possible in the context of democratically inclusive institutions, the bicameral system, proportional elections, and decentralization, which offered the decisive possibilities for rule-based and long-lasting conflict management. The interplay of external pressure and monitoring, integration into European and interregional networks, and the leadership role of non-nationalist and left-wing minority-friendly parties had, as argued, an additional positive impact on the process of ethnic recognition and the consolidation of the autonomy system.

In contrast, the reason for the failure of the CHT autonomy arrangement is the toxic interplay of different unfavorable conditions that reactivated the grievance-conflict path and led to renewed ethnic mobilization. The 1997 CHT agreement contains only comparatively weak self-rule powers, which were also not fully implemented. The regional institutions are dominated by Bengali representatives and serve merely for control and co-optation. The peace negotiations were kept highly exclusive and no timetable or interim evaluation has been carried out, leading to constant disputes over responsibilities. The lack of self-determination and political inclusion gave rise to a feeling of continued heteronomy and an enforced, Bengali-controlled political system. The criticism of the insufficient degree of autonomy and the resulting elite split is a further burden for peaceful ethnic cohabitation. The group members supported the elites in their course of confrontation and the non-acceptance of the autonomy reforms. As postulated by the theoretical model, this can be traced back to strong horizontal inequalities between majority and minority, which are found in both the economic and social dimensions. The resulting grievances are constantly instrumentalized by ethnic leaders, which results in a vicious circle of violence and counter-violence. The blame game is fostered by the nationalist parties in the central state, which strongly adhere to exclusive and anti-multicultural nationalism and show little willingness to recognize the Jumma minority as constitutive part of the demos. The political regime offers hardly any opportunities for conventional political participation and peaceful cooperation but instead fosters arbitrary rule and repression.

References

Achankeng, Fonkem. *Nationalism and Intra-State Conflicts in the Postcolonial World*. London: Lexington Books, 2015.

Barkat, Abdul, Sadeka Halim, Mohammad Badiuzzaman, Asmar Osman, Shahnewaz Khan, Matiur Rahman, Murtaza Majid, Golam Mahiyuddin, Sushmita Chakma, and Sharmina Bashir. *Socio-Economic Baseline Survey of Chittagong Hill Tracts*. Prepared for Chittagong Hill Tracts Development Facility. Dhaka, 2009.

Barkat, Abdul, Avijit Poddar, Mohammad Badiuzzaman, and Asmar Osman. "Situation Analysis of Chittagong Hill Tracts in Bangladesh. An Analysis Based on 'Socio-Economic Baseline Survey of Chittagong Hill Tracts' Data." Human Development Research Center, 2008.

Beach, Derek, and Ingo Rohlfing. "Integrating Cross-Case Analyses and Process Tracing in Set-Theoretic Research: Strategies and Parameters of Debate." *Sociological Methods & Research*, 47, no. 1 (2018): 3–36.

Chakma, Saradindu Shekhar. *Ethnic Cleansing in Chittagong Hill Tracts*. Dhaka: Ankur Prakashani, 2006.

Chittagong Hill Tracts Accord. "Chittagong Hill Tracts Peace Accord," 1997. https://peaceaccords.nd.edu.

Ferrandi, Giuseppe, Günther Pallaver, and Andrea Leonardi. *La regione Trentino-Alto Adige*. Trento: Museo storico in Trento, 2007.

Grote, Georg. *I bin a Südtiroler: Kollektive Identität zwischen Nation und Region im 20. Jahrhundert*. Bozen: Athesia, 2009.

Marko, Joseph, Francesco Palermo, and Jens Woelk, eds. *Tolerance through Law. Self-Governance and Group Rights in South Tyrol*. Leiden: Brill, 2007.

Mohsin, Amena. *Conflict and Partition: Chittagong Hill Tracts, Bangladesh*. Edited by Delwar Hossain. Los Angeles: SAGE Publications, 2015.

Pallaver, Günther. "South Tyrol's Changing Political System: From Dissociative on the Road to Associative Conflict Resolution." *Nationalities Papers* 42, no. 3 (2014): 376–398.

PCJSS. "UNPO: Chittagong Hill Tracts: PCJSS Statement on 20th Anniversary of CHT Accord (Jyotirindra Bodhipriya Larma)." Unrepresented Nations & Peoples Organization, 2017. http://unpo.org/article/20495 (June 2017).

Provincial Administration South Tyrol. " 20 Jahre Europa-Angelegenheiten. Direkter Draht zur EU," 2011. http://www.provinz.bz.it/ (September 2017).

Provincial Statistics Institute South Tyrol. "Jugendstudie. Werthaltungen, Lebensformen und Lebensentwürfe der Südtiroler Jugend." ASTAT, 2017.

———. "Südtiroler Sprachbarometer. Barometro Linguistico Dell'Alto Adige. Sprachgebrauch und Sprachidentität in Südtirol." ASTAT, 2005.

———. "Südtiroler Sprachbarometer. Barometro Linguistico Dell'Alto Adige. Sprachgebrauch und Sprachidentität in Südtirol." ASTAT, 2015a.

———. "Zufriedenheit der Bürger mit den Öffentlichen Diensten." ASTAT, 2015b.

Solderer, Gottfried, and Siglinde Clementi, eds. *Das 20. Jahrhundert in Südtirol. Autonomie und Aufbruch*. Vol. 4. Bozen: Edition Rætia, 1999.

Südtiroler Volkspartei. "Das neue Programm der Südtiroler Volkspartei beschlossen von der Landesversammlung am 8. Mai 1993." SVP, Meran, 1993. www.svp.eu (August 2017).

UPDF. "United Peoples Democratic Front Manifesto," 1998. http://updfcht.com/ (September 2017)

Zappe, Manuela. *Das ethnische Zusammenleben in Südtirol: sprachsoziologische, sprachpolitische und soziokulturelle Einstellungen der deutschen, italienischen und ladinischen Sprachgruppe vor und nach den gegenwärtigen Umbrüchen in Europa*. Frankfurt a. M.: Peter Lang, 1996.

Zeitgeschichte Informationssystem. "22./23.11.1969: Auszug der 18-Stunden-Debatte der SVP-Landesversammlung in Meran." https://www.uibk.ac.at/ (August 2018).

CHAPTER 5

Conclusion: Increasing the Chances of Autonomy Success

Ethnic conflicts are undoubtedly one of the prevailing challenges to international security, democracy, and development in our time.[1] An aspect of civil wars to consider is why they start. The other—even more challenging—aspect is how they can be ended. Conflicts as social interactions are changeable. This also holds true for highly emotional cultural conflicts over ethnic and national identity, recognition, and political participation. Ethnic peace is not the result of an invisible hand, but rather of an emerging regime of managing institutions that are able to transform majority-minority conflicts into peaceful interethnic cohabitation. The specific design of political institutions shapes the incentives of actors, constraints their actions, and creates stimuli for cooperative behavior.

Bloody civil wars in Bosnia, Rwanda, and elsewhere have not only made international peacebuilders become increasingly engaged in institutional reforms as a promising medication to foster the nonviolent management of intrastate conflicts, but have also stimulated a lively debate in academia on which specific design makes state institutions work for peace and democracy. While the general importance of institutions is widely accepted among scholars, the specific effects of different institutional designs on peace processes are highly contested. Scholars have not yet found a reliable answer to the question of which institutional reforms work best under which circumstances for building peace in multi-ethnic societies. Some

[1] Cordell and Wolff, *The Routledge Handbook of Ethnic Conflict*, 1.

F. Schulte, *Peace through Self-Determination*, Federalism and Internal Conflicts,
https://doi.org/10.1007/978-3-030-37587-4_5

approaches seem to have worked in regulating ethnic rivalries in some places while others seem to be at odds with difficult realities on the ground.

An ongoing scholarly debate between consociationalists and centripetalists concerns the wisdom of recognizing versus avoiding the recognition of ethnic identities in post-war institutions. Some scholars make the case that centripetal institutions such as instant-runoff voting reduce the political salience of cultural groups and are best to regulate severe ethnic tensions. This study has built on socio-psychological assumptions and intergroup behavior and has made a strong point for the consociational strand of research. As subordination along ethnic lines provides new causes for intergroup conflict, consociationalism emphasizes the need to recognize group identities through governmental concessions, for example, in the form of regional autonomy, executive power sharing, or protective group rights.

This book has brought territorial autonomy arrangements to the fore, a subnational type sui generis that has hitherto only been given insufficient consideration in recent literature. Territorial autonomies are based on the principle of a vertical division of political powers, and, therefore, cannot be subsumed under the concept of power sharing as is frequently done in relevant literature. This book has defined territorial autonomy as a legally guaranteed special status with exclusive executive and legislative rights. The concept must be distinguished from symmetrical guaranteed or non-guaranteed standard entities such as federalism and decentralization but also from other subnational forms with special status but without any legal guarantee, such as devolution or non-territorial autonomy.

In the light of settled minority conflicts in Åland, South Tyrol, or elsewhere, many scholars have strongly argued for autonomy reforms to regulate ethnic self-determination conflicts. According to the proponents, self-rule reduces the stakes of competition for state power which in turn prevents the mutual exploitation of rival groups. Separate institutions on regional level allow for a balance "between the common and the particular", ensure official recognition and substantial self-government for ethnic groups, and, in turn, reduce their separatist desires.[2] At the same time, autonomy solutions take the sovereignty and territorial integrity as key political interests a nation-state into account, without, however, being dependent on functioning cooperation in grand coalitions.

[2] Ghai, *Autonomy and Ethnicity. Negotiating Competing Claims in Multi-Ethnic States*, 24.

As this book has shown, autonomy reforms do not have a too "terrible track record" when it comes to ethnic conflict regulation.[3] Nevertheless, many authors seem to have been overly optimistic and have underestimated certain realities on the ground. Post-conflict autonomy reforms do not bridge cultural cleavages, but rather institutionalize them. The asymmetric and exclusive character of territorial self-government has led to a strong accentuation of ethnic differences in almost all autonomous regions of the sample, especially when territorial autonomy is combined with subnational power sharing such as in Northern Ireland, Iraqi Kurdistan, or New Caledonia. Empowerments offers access to financial resources and mass media, and it is usually not very difficult to find external support by diaspora groups or kin states for their struggle for independence. Developments in the Spanish regions, for example, show that it is then an easy task for ethnic leaders to put separatist demands on the political agenda and mobilize deprived group members.

Post-conflict institutional engineering can even have perverse effects, as it sometimes can produce new conflicts. With that being said, both institutional successes and failures do not occur in a vacuum. They rather depend on both the right choice of institutional design, as well as certain external factors. Each peace process is unique, but the real challenge for social scientists and policymakers is to untangle the conditions that are common in the simultaneous breakdown of institutional arrangements and the consolidation of others.

This study has addressed this central shortcoming in the existing literature, which has focused primarily on a general performance potential of conflict-regulating autonomies or executive power sharing agreements or the effect of single exogenous or endogenous variables on the re-occurrence of ethnic violence. The book has introduced a comprehensive theory that explains why some post-conflict territorial autonomy arrangements have consolidated and have managed to ease ethnic tensions while others have failed to do so. Based on Social Identity Theory, it was argued that people strive for the recognition of their personal and social identities and cannot be persuaded to abandon the satisfaction of this basic human need. Ethnic groups whose social identity is based on life-determining cultural elements, such as language, customs, historical experiences, or religion, have a particularly high need for recognition from others. Regardless of physical resources or political power, ethnic identity groups

[3] Snyder, *From Voting to Violence*, 327.

will agitate, though in different ways, for the satisfaction of those basic needs. Ethnic self-determination conflicts are essentially cultural identity conflicts for cultural recognition.

In line with this socio-psychological approach, ethnic recognition, defined as the mutual acceptance of cultural differences without devaluation, is to be regarded the all-important key for successful ethnic conflict regulation. Autonomy arrangements are, at least theoretically, suitable institutions for ethnic conflict regulation because they provide for minority recognition through a special status and a substantial degree of self-determination. However, mutual recognition between former belligerents as key prerequisite for autonomy success, or consolidation, is highly difficult and anything but easy to achieve. To explain the variance in consolidation outcome, a theoretical approach was developed that takes into account both collective identities as well as various exogenous factors.

The book argued that successful autonomy consolidation phases include a three-stage social mechanism resulting in ethnic recognition: To start, the autonomy solution must be widely accepted as the rules of the game by ethnic elites. Ethnic leaders support institutional reforms if these reforms credibly promise real empowerment and, consequently, political power. The chances of achieving self-determination are higher than the chances of alternative strategies of gaining influence being successful. At the same time, though, ethnic leaders need the support of ordinary group members. Both factions share the primary interest in empowerment and recognition, whereas elites act as the agents of general group interest. Ordinary group members are more accepting of institutional reforms when they expect them to improve their lives and have a credible commitment that self-determination rights and cultural protection will continue in the future and will not be replaced by majority dominance and assimilation efforts. Ethnic recognition presupposes that this general acceptance leads to cooperation and rapprochement among elites. The vague acceptance of the institutional framework is followed by specific cooperation efforts and elite pacts, but only if suitable cooperation opportunities are available to the actors in addition to sufficient incentives and pressures to adhere to the agreements. Successful cooperation at the political level then sends decisive signals for rapprochement processes on societal level. This ultimately enables broad mutual recognition and ensures the consolidation of the autonomy arrangement.

The central puzzle to be solved is how exactly this mechanism is initiated and upheld in diverse contexts. A cross-case comparison of consolidation outcomes has shown that individual factors cannot fully explain the variance in consolidation outcomes. This explains why most studies have found only weak statistical effects of variables such as the quality of liberal democracy, rule of law, or group size. It was concluded that it is not specific factors, but rather a particular configuration of several conditions, both structural and actor centered, that contribute to autonomy success or failure. On the basis of identity-theoretical considerations, seven success factors were identified: an adequate de facto degree of self-determination, a peaceful and non-secessionist conflict strategy, democratization of the central state, the absence of severe social and economic inequalities between majority and minority, as well as internationalization in the form of the engagement of international organizations and the international integration of the region. The application of fuzzy-set QCA as a variable-oriented and cross-case method reveals that almost all successful cases show a high degree of self-rule. Supplemented by the conditions of democratization and international integration, this provides a minimal and sufficient explanation for the success of the European autonomies Åland, Basque Country, New Caledonia, Gagauzia, and South Tyrol.

To broaden the range of the explanation, with the rule of law, the national electoral system, the degree of decentralization, the existence of nationalist parties and diaspora groups, as well as ethnic fractionalization, six additional factors were included and analyzed. As expected, the rule of law, decentralization, and systems of proportional representation as well as the existence of nationalist parties are indeed important for explaining the phenomenon. Contrary to what many authors suspect, ethnic fragmentation and the existence of diaspora groups play only a minor role for autonomy consolidation.

In a second empirical step, all relevant conditions were combined into two empirical models. The model of success explains autonomy consolidation through a fruitful interplay of weak horizontal inequalities, a high degree of autonomy, democratic-inclusive institutions, minority-friendly parties, and international support. Autonomy reforms that contain only a limited degree of self-rule for a marginalized minority and that are introduced to regulate a highly violent secessionist conflict in an undemocratic environment without any external support are doomed for failure. QCA confirms that these conjunctions are indeed sufficient to explain the consolidation of at least most of the relevant cases. The results remain highly robust with other calibration decisions and data.

In a second step, the empirical models were provided with empirical implications about the causal influence of the identified factors on the proposed three-stage social mechanism of ethnic recognition. According to the theoretical assumptions, it should be observable that a high degree of autonomy rights and low social and economic intergroup inequalities increase the acceptance of autonomy reforms. Democratically inclusive institutions and minority-friendly parties as well as international support should promote elite cooperation and provide decisive impulses for social rapprochement processes. Conversely, it was expected that an inadequate degree of self-rule and political exclusion results in a broad rejection of institutional reforms. This, in turn, leads to dangerous grievances when there are strong social or economic horizontal asymmetries between majority and minority. A lack of democracy and an absence of international support, as well as the polarizing effect of nationalist parties, then fuel ongoing ethnic conflict.

To test the two causal models, two representative cases were selected: first, South Tyrol in Northern Italy, which has been granted autonomy in 1972 and today can look back on 25 years of ethnic peace. After almost 50 years of simmering conflict, a state of mutual recognition between Germans, Italians, and Ladins has developed, mediated by an autonomy system and brought about by favorable recognition-enabling factors. The case study finds evidence that the extensive powers included in the package deal convinced the SVP elites in South Tyrol. The combination of international pressure from the United Nations, inclusive cooperation-arenas, and minority-friendly parties at central and substate level fostered continuous cooperation between the SVP and the central government in Rome. The once omnipresent discourse of marginalization and repression among the South Tyroleans has gradually diminished through de facto empowerment and the absence of horizontal inequalities, allowing the masses to support the elites in their policy of rapprochement. Second, the Chittagong Hill Tracts (CHT), which were declared an autonomous region with the 1997 peace treaty, but where the institutional reforms could not end the almost 50-year struggle of the ethnic Jumma against the Bengali majority population. The case study has illustrated the vicious circle of violence and counter-violence, initiated by deep mistrust and grievances, which are constantly instrumentalized by ethnic demagogues. Ethnic leaders did not universally accept the autonomy offer due to the very low level of transferred political, financial, and cultural powers and ongoing political exclusion from national decision-making processes. The poorly implemented reforms did not bring the Jumma any improvement in their living conditions in the remote villages. This produced new grievances among the local population and led to a broad rejection of the CHT peace treaty. While the Awami League (AL) and the Bangladesh Nationalist Party (BNP) as authoritarian-nationalist parties continue to fuel the cultural conflict, neither the political system nor international actors help to weaken ethnic tensions. Both case studies find strong evidence for the established causal models.

Scientific research is a catalyst for solving complex practical issues. The very raison d' être for peace and conflict studies is to develop the necessary knowledge needed to end devastating ethnic conflicts and to create peace. As far as is known, this book provides the first comprehensive theory to explain the success and failure of territorial autonomy as a promising option to end ethnic conflict. The study not only gives an explanation of which conditions are crucial, but also how different structural and actor-centered factors interact within an institutional framework of vertical power division. The causal models can thus serve as political orientation frameworks for international actors or central governments to enhance the consolidation chances of post-conflict autonomy reforms.

The fostering of democratic governance and the rule of law is a standard prescription for peacemakers around the world. Furthermore, efforts by international organizations or NGOs in post-conflict societies almost always involve reducing regional disparities. There is little scholarly controversy that these two conditions significantly increase the chances of sustainable peace, which is also the case when conflict resolution involves institutional reforms. What is important, as mentioned above, is not so much the absolute level of participation and inequality as continuous progress in these sectors. There are dozens of examples of how democracy promotion and the reduction of inequalities can succeed in ethnically divided societies, and that even small improvements can have a substantial impact on human development. Needless to say, that these are long-term goals that cannot be achieved overnight, but take years, sometimes decades, of continuous effort. However, the analysis has detected other conditions that are easier to change and to shape politically. They entail lower costs but are equally significant in their impact. At least three important lessons can be drawn from the empirical analysis as to how to increase the consolidation chances of conflict-regulating territorial autonomies. These lessons concern the degree of self-determination, the creation of stable and predictable communication platforms, and the role of external mediators and international attention to ethnic self-determination movements in peripheral regions.

Transfer of the Highest Possible Scope of Autonomy

A main empirical finding of the study is that a high degree of self-determination is a quasi-necessary condition for autonomy success. Almost all consolidated autonomies enjoy a comparatively high degree of self-determination that includes political, financial, and cultural powers. Also, the timing of the transfer of competences plays an important role. In Åland, South Tyrol, or Gagauzia, territorial self-government was offered before ethnic tensions completely escalated and the conflict became intractable. The autonomy arrangement was then gradually developed, whereas the central governments responded adequately and flexibly to new political challenges without recentralizing powers.

In contrast, the cases of Northern Ireland, Mindanao, or Chittagong Hill Tracts show that inadequate or too late autonomy offers can lead to a security dilemma that can easily escalate and is extremely difficult to stop. The most fear-producing scenario occurs for groups when autonomy rights once transferred are withdrawn or suspended. Both currently autonomous and never autonomous ethnic groups are much less likely to fight secessionist wars than groups that once enjoyed self-determination but have lost their special status.[4] The suspension of the special status for Kashmir by the nationalist Indian government in August 2019 does not augur well for the region and the already fragile peace between the Hindu majority and Kashmiris. Self-determination groups will do their utmost to achieve a positive group status. The costs of transferring far-reaching competencies to the subnational level are obviously much lower for a central government than offering only insufficient autonomy or not fully implement territorial self-government, thus risking the emergence of an intractable ethnic conflict that generates heavy economic and political costs.

[4] Siroky and Cuffe, "Lost Autonomy, Nationalism and Separatism."

Continuously Maintaining the Process of Mutual Recognition

Ethnic recognition is always a work in progress. It is a complex, multidimensional, and not necessarily convergent process. Even in many consolidated autonomies such as Åland or South Tyrol, right-wing nationalist parties have entered the regional assemblies. In Catalonia, Iraqi Kurdistan, and most recently New Caledonia, secessionist parties have initiated highly controversial referendums on independence. In order to avoid perceived identity threats and dangerous security dilemmas, constant efforts and offers are needed to maintain the process of mutual recognition. A short comparison of recent political developments in two successful cases of the sample, Catalonia and South Tyrol, illustrates how such offers can look like and how dangerous it is when such are missing.

After the elections in 2003, the main objective of the Catalan government was to reform the special status that had been granted in 1979. The "procés" seemed to be on the right path in 2004 when Socialist candidate, José L. R. Zapatero, declared that he was willing to accept a new statute for the region. A year later, the regional parliament approved a proposal, which included demands to state that Catalonia is a nation, to make Catalan the public language in the region, and to increase tax-collecting powers.[5]

The proposal was sent to the Spanish parliament, which, however, modified different clauses, including the nation-paragraph. Nevertheless, in a plebiscite held in 2006 to ratify the amendments, the Catalans approved the new statute. Since most Catalans were quite satisfied with their entity's federal nature at that time, turnout in the referendum was low. Things began to change when the Partido Popular Party (PP) appealed the approval of the new statute at the constitutional court. The PP even went so far as to collect millions of signatures from across the entire country against the new autonomy statute. The minority conflict began to gain momentum again when the Spanish High Court of Justice ruled that key articles of the statute were unconstitutional, which rendered the amendments meaningless. Among the Catalans, the feeling of a continuous erosion of their self-government grew considerably. Deprivation was fueled by the Euro crisis and economic recession that hit the region in 2008. Unemployment rose from about 7 percent in 2007 to 17.75 percent

[5] Kraus and Gifra, *The Catalan Process.*

in 2010.[6] Local politicians attributed the fact that other regions, such as the Basque country, were not hit that hard to the lack of financial competencies, refused by the state authorities. The nationalist agenda of central state parties gave secessionist aspirations a further boost. For example, Catalonia's ban on bullfighting was overturned in 2010 in order to "preserve the common cultural heritage" of the country.

Backed by growing mass rallies, pro-independence parties won a majority in the regional assembly and adopted a "Sovereignty Declaration" in 2013, asserting that the minority group had the right to decide on its own political future. After the 2015 elections, the regional government declared the start of the independence process and the new Catalan president, Carles Puigdemont, announced a binding referendum on independence, which was, although again ruled unconstitutional, held in October 2017. Results showed a 90 percent support for secession, with a turnout of 43 percent.[7] Based on this popular support, Puigdemont declared the full independence of the autonomous region, but left it suspended. During the referendum there were some violent clashes between state police forces and pro-independence activists, prompting the national government to disempower the regional government and to arrest some of its members.

Although the Italian government faced similar economic and demographic challenges, it was able to prevent the flare-up of ethnic tensions in their autonomous regions. In these cases, recent regional reform efforts were approached in a participatory and inclusive manner, stimulating the process of mutual recognition. In 2013, the South Tyrolean government announced a participatory reform process to revise the 1972 statute and to secure legitimacy for negotiations with the central government. As in Catalonia, the reform process was seen as a response to successive pushes by the central government to re-centralize powers. The participatory process, the so-called Autonomy Convention, included not only members of the German and Ladin minority but also Italian citizens. The Convention, which started in 2016, had three main components, the first being discussion rounds where all citizens of the region had the opportunity to speak their mind and offer and discuss suggestions on how to revise South Tyrol's special autonomy statute, second the "Forum of 100", and third, the "Convention of 33". The Forum served as some kind of a temporary

[6] Idescat Catalonia, "Idescat. Demographics and Quality of Life. At Risk of Poverty or Social Exclusion (Europe 2020 Strategy) and Its Components. Base 2013. Results."

[7] Institut d'Estadistica de Catalunya, "Basic Data Statistics."

citizens' assembly whose members were chosen in proportion to their ethnicity, age, and gender. The latter served as the joint decision-making body of the language groups and was made up of 33 politicians and civil society actors.[8]

The Convention registered a high level of participation, successfully brought all ethnic groups to the table to discuss their common political future and was another important step to overcome the group boundaries. A final policy paper to amend the autonomy statute was prepared and sent to the regional parliament for submission to the Italian government as a basis for further negotiations. As a result of the moderating reform processes, separatist parties such as Die Freiheitlichen or Süd-Tiroler Freiheit suffered considerable losses of votes in the last regional elections in both autonomous regions.

In addition to the recommendations given to affected central governments to guarantee a high degree of self-rule at an early stage and to maintain the process of recognition on an ongoing basis, the third and final policy recommendation is addressed to the international community.

International Intervention

International organizations have become more ambitious in regulating intrastate conflicts since the end of the Cold War. Compared to the Pre-Cold War period when about 4 percent of Civil War years experienced international mediation, the ratio in the new millennium was nearly four times as high.[9] The total number of ongoing international peace operations worldwide in mid-2019 stood at 71.[10] Of these, about one-third were deployed in conflicts that include one or more cultural identity groups and, thus, are to be declared as ethnic conflicts according to the definition introduced above. Well-known examples include the UN Kashmir Mission (UNMOGIP), the EU Mission in Ukraine (EUAM), or the OSCE missions in Kosovo and Bosnia-Herzegovina.

As outlined above, external actors have a wide range of powerful intervention options and regulation instruments at hand, ranging from

[8] Larin and Röggla, "South Tyrol's Autonomy Convention Is Not a Breakthrough for Participatory Democracy—But It Shows How Power-Sharing Can Transform Conflicts"; Alber and Woelk, "Autonomie (Reform) 2.0."

[9] Wallensteen and Svensson, "Talking Peace."

[10] Center for International Peace Operations, "Peace Operations 2018/2019."

diplomatic measures aimed at inducing parties to reach a settlement to security sector reforms, institutional capacity building or, as ultima ratio, the use of military force.

Current international peace operations in ethnic conflicts vary in length, costs, equipment, objectives—and success. We should bear in mind that not every international intervention per se aims to resolve a conflict peacefully by mutual agreement. Consequences, intended or unintended, may produce outcomes not conducive to, or even hampering, peaceful ethnic coexistence. It is also clear that international interventions are no guarantee for sustainable conflict regulation. This study has demonstrated that the involvement of international organizations in peace negotiations alone is neither a necessary nor a sufficient condition for the success of conflict-regulating autonomy reforms. Similar findings can also be expected for the likelihood of consolidation of other post-conflict institutions such as decentralization, executive power sharing, or electoral reforms.

However, peace research has found that international involvement can be effective, even in cases with a high structural risk of conflict re-occurrence, caused by previous conflict experiences, deprivation and low development, or bad neighborhoods. Despite cases of blatant disasters, such as the failure of the UN missions to prevent the genocides against the Tutsis or Bosniaks in the 1990s, research finds strong correlations of mediation success, including limiting human rights violations and reducing the likelihood of conflict re-occurrence. Post-conflict countries that receive substantial international support have a higher chance of a peaceful future than countries that are largely neglected by the international community.[11]

International mediation is usually a comparatively inexpensive investment that makes ethnic peace at least a little more likely. Case reports of Aceh, Bougainville, or South Tyrol in this book have shown that intervention has often succeeded in at least encouraging moves by ethnic rebels and central governments toward peace talks and reducing ethnic violence to a more manageable level. As (often) neutral mediators, international organizations can contribute to finding sustainable solutions and can exert diplomatic, economic or military pressure on conflict parties to abide by agreements and can help to forestall that ethnic demagogues, diasporas, or

[11] Fiedler, Grävingholt, and Mross, "Supporting Peace after Civil War"; Smidt, "United Nations Peacekeeping Locally"; Lundgren, "Which Type of International Organizations Can Settle Civil Wars?"

kin states with their own power interests produce protracted and highly insecure conflict environments.

The study has shown that this positive effect also applies to the integration of autonomous regions into international or regional networks, a success factor that has so far been largely unnoticed in literature. The long-term international integration of an autonomous region can serve, on the one hand, as an additional communication channel in times of crisis and may help with economic and social recovery, especially in peripheral regions. On the other hand, integration is, and this seems to be much more important, a form of external recognition and a certain guarantee of a special autonomy status. The examples of South Tyrol's integration in regional networks such as the ArgeAlp, the Euroregion Tyrol-South Tyrol-Trentino, and the European Union or Åland in the Nordic Council and the Baltic Sea Parliamentary Conference, demonstrate that international integration can even be an attractive alternative to costly independence demands.

Also, the international integration of post-conflict autonomies alone is neither a necessary nor a sufficient condition but part of a conjunction of different structural and actor-centered success factors. But this favorable condition is comparatively inexpensive, less conflict-laden, and in many cases less politically controversial, and still increases the chance of ethnic peace. The institutional network of the European Union, for example, offers hitherto untapped opportunities for a stronger integration of minority regions, such as the Székely Land or Silesia.

The study offers some fruitful avenues for further research on post-conflict institutional engineering. The study considers only territorial autonomies and has used a comparatively narrow definition for case selection. The results are therefore not directly transferable to other managing institutions and empirical findings. The elaborated causal models, which have only been tested on basis of two typical cases, need to prove its reliability in further studies focusing on decentralization or power sharing reforms.

Furthermore, the outcomes of success and failure were measured at a fixed time, which results in consolidation periods of different durations and implies a bias at the expense of younger arrangements. However, the longer a peace process lasts, the greater the chances of its success. Despite some adjustments to the democratization and inequality condition, the temporal dimension was only insufficiently taken into account in the QCA analyses and was therefore not thoroughly incorporated into the causal models. Although the case studies confirm the basic assumption that the conditions affect institutional consolidation at different times, it remains unclear whether an autonomy arrangement has gone through several phases and was once successful and then later failed or vice versa and whether such processes were hindered or fostered by the identified conditions or other variables, such as the internal fragmentation of self-determination movements, lost historical self-government, state capacity, or the strategic importance of the autonomous territory for the central government.

As some critics argue, autonomy reforms set up institutions and resources that are tapped by secessionists in order to support renewed fighting with the government if their secessionist demands are not satisfied. In some cases of the sample, an escalation of ethnic violence can indeed be observed shortly after an autonomy offer has been made by the central government. But which cases are recovering, and which are not? This begs the important question of how and why autonomy crises arise in consolidated cases, which autonomy crises lead to autonomy failure and which circumstances drive these processes. Since the conditions of the theoretical model are all interdependent, successful autonomies may backslide if one or more success factors "break off" after a while. Recent developments in Catalonia provide, as illustrated above, some indications for this hypothesis.

The biggest challenge for future research, though, will be to connect various structural factors on different levels, the behavior, instrumentalizations and manipulations of local elites, and collective actions of self-determination organizations in a theoretically meaningful way. The logic of institutional approaches implies that also the specific set-up at regional and local level provides incentives and constraints for political action and is therefore decisive for consolidation processes. This applies to the combination of territorial self-governance and power sharing in Northern Ireland or South Tyrol, to incorporated traditional institutions in Bougainville or mediation committees in Åland. Here, too, more research is needed.

Territorial autonomy is not a relevant option for alleviating tensions between ethnic groups in all contexts. Where groups are geographically intermingled or equally powerful, territorial self-government may not be the best option for managing interethnic tensions. However, most ethnic conflicts worldwide revolve around self-determination demands of minorities in majority-dominated and unitary nation-states. For these "classical" ethnic conflicts, regional autonomy is often more than just a relevant option—it may be the only realistic option in the menu of institutional engineering that can bring ethnic war to an end. Ongoing ethnic wars in East Ukraine, Northern Syria, or elsewhere are unlikely to be regulated peacefully without some form of political autonomy and many of the world's various breakaway regions like Transnistria, Abkhazia, or Nagorno-Karabakh are unlikely to re-join their parent state under any institutional design other than territorial self-government. However, for any medication prescribed to a patient, the side effects and chances of recovery should be known. The study has yielded some important findings in this regard for a promising institution to encourage peace in deeply divided societies.

References

Alber, Elisabeth, and Jens Woelk. "Autonomie (Reform) 2.0: Parallele Verfahren partizipativer Demokratie. Zur Reform des Autonomiestatuts der Region Trentino-Südtirol." In *Jahrbuch des Föderalismus 2018*, 172–188. Baden-Baden: Nomos, 2018.

Center for International Peace Operations, Center for International Peace. "Peace Operations 2018/2019." Peace Operations 2018/2019, 2019. https://www.zif-berlin.org/en.html (June 2019).

Cordell, Karl, and Stefan Wolff, eds. *The Routledge Handbook of Ethnic Conflict*. 2nd edn. London: Routledge, 2016.

Fiedler, Charlotte, Jörn Grävingholt, and Karina Mross. "Supporting Peace after Civil War: What Kind of International Engagement Can Make a Difference?" German Development Institute Briefing Paper, 2018.

Ghai, Yash. *Autonomy and Ethnicity. Negotiating Competing Claims in Multi-Ethnic States*. Cambridge: Cambridge University Press, 2000.

Idescat Catalonia. "Idescat. Demographics and Quality of Life. At Risk of Poverty or Social Exclusion (Europe 2020 Strategy) and Its Components," 2016. http://www.idescat.cat/ (November 2016).

Institut d'Estadistica de Catalunya. "Basic Data Statistics," 2017. http://www.idescat.cat/ (December 2017).

Kraus, Peter A., and Joan Vergés Gifra, eds. *The Catalan Process: Sovereignty, Self-Determination and Democracy in the 21st Century*. Barcelona: Generalitat de Catalunya, Institut d'Estudis de l'Autogovern, 2017.

Larin, Steven, and Marc Röggla. "South Tyrol's Autonomy Convention Is Not a Breakthrough for Participatory Democracy—But It Shows How Power-Sharing Can Transform Conflicts." LSE. EUROPP, 2016. http://blogs.lse.ac.uk/.

Lundgren, Magnus. "Which Type of International Organizations Can Settle Civil Wars?" *The Review of International Organizations* 12, no. 4 (2017): 613–641.

Siroky, David S., and John Cuffe. "Lost Autonomy, Nationalism and Separatism." *Comparative Political Studies* 48, no. 1 (2015): 3–34.

Smidt, Hannah M. "United Nations Peacekeeping Locally: Enabling Conflict Resolution, Reducing Communal Violence." *Journal of Conflict Resolution*, 2019 (Online First). https://doi.org/10.1177/0022002719859631.

Snyder, Jack L. *From Voting to Violence: Democratization and Nationalist Conflict*. New York: Norton, 2000.

Wallensteen, Peter, and Isak Svensson. "Talking Peace: International Mediation in Armed Conflicts." *Journal of Peace Research* 51, no. 2 (2014): 315–327.

Index[1]

[1] Note: Page numbers followed by 'n' refer to notes.

F. Schulte, *Peace through Self-Determination*, Federalism and Internal Conflicts,
https://doi.org/10.1007/978-3-030-37587-4

T